"Hope always draws the soul from the beauty which is seen to what is beyond, always kindles the desire for the hidden through what is constantly perceived. Therefore, the ardent lover of beauty, although receiving what is always visible as an image of what he desires, yet longs to be filled with the very stamp of the archetype."

GREGORY OF NYSSA

THE UNCREATED
LIGHT

An Iconographical Study
of the Transfiguration
in the Eastern Church

SOLRUNN NES

translated by
ARLYNE MOI

WILLIAM B. EERDMANS PUBLISHING COMPANY
GRAND RAPIDS, MICHIGAN / CAMBRIDGE, U.K.

First published in Norwegian as *Det Uskapte Lyset:*
Ein ikonografisk studie av Transfigurasjonsmotivet i Austkyrkja by Solum Forlag
First published in English 2002 by Eastern Christian Publications
Translated from the Norwegian by Arlyne Moi

This edition published 2007 by Wm. B. Eerdmans Publishing Co.
2140 Oak Industrial Drive N.E., Grand Rapids, Michigan 49505 /
P.O. Box 163, Cambridge CB3 9PU U.K.

Printed in the United States of America

12 11 10 09 08 07   7 6 5 4 3 2 1

Library of Congress Cataloging-in-Publication Data

Nes, Solrunn.
[Uskapte lyset. English]
The uncreated light: an iconographical study of the
transfiguration in the Eastern Church / Solrunn Nes.
p.   cm.
Includes bibliographical references.
ISBN 978-0-8028-1764-8 (cloth: alk. paper)
1. Jesus Christ — Transfiguration. 2. Jesus Christ — Transfiguration — Art.
3. Orthodox Eastern Church — Doctrines. 4. Image (Theology)
5. Hesychasm. 6. Orthodox Eastern Church — In art.   I. Title

BT410.N4713   2007

232.9′56 — dc22

2007007770

www.eerdmans.com

to my mother

CONTENTS

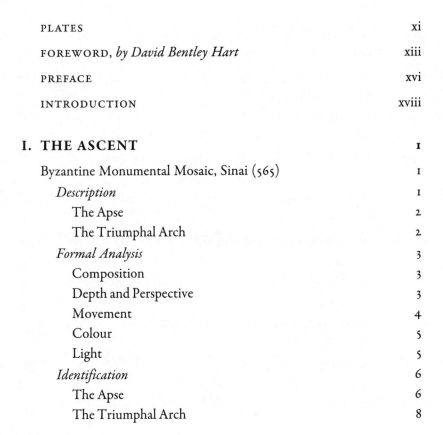

Contents

PLATES

FOREWORD

In the icon of Christ's transfiguration upon Mount Tabor—as in the feast of light to which it is liturgically attached—the entire "logic" of Eastern Christian theology, devotion, worship, and mysticism is uniquely concentrated. This is not to say that the icon is either aesthetically or doctrinally more important than any number of other canonical Byzantine icons, such as that of the risen Lord liberating souls from Hades, or that of the Crucifixion, or that of the Mother of God with the infant Christ in her arms, and so on; but it is to say that, as an object of contemplation, the Transfiguration image comprises within itself the whole story of creation, incarnation, and salvation in a particular way, with a special harmony of elements, and with a singular intensity. It allows us, in one fixed instant of visionary clarity, to see and to reflect upon the entire mystery of the God-man and of the divinization of our humanity in Him. The light that radiates from the figure of Christ is the eternal glory of His godhead shining through—and entirely pervading—His flesh. It is the visible beauty of the glory that entered the world to tabernacle among us in the Person of the eternal Son: the same glory that passed through the history of Israel, that transfigured the face of Moses, that dwelt in the Temple in Jerusalem, that rested upon the Mercy Seat of the Ark of the Covenant, that overshadowed Mary when the angel of God appeared to her, and that has at various times throughout the history of the Church revealed itself to and in the saints.

The icon also, however, offers us a glimpse of the eschatological horizon of salvation; for the same light that the three disciples were permitted to see break forth from the body of Christ will, in the fullness of time, enter into and transform all of creation, with that glory that the Son had with the Father before the world began (John 17:5), and that the whole of creation awaits with groans of longing and travail (Rom. 8:19-23). Then, to use an image favored by a host of Orthodox spiritual writers, the entire universe will be like the burning bush seen by Moses: radiant with the fire of God's holiness, but not consumed. And the Christian who prayerfully turns his gaze to the Transfiguration icon, and holds it there, should see himself taken up into the incarnate God, and refashioned after the ancient beauty of the divine image. For, just as it is Christ's humanity that is transfigured in the light of his divinity, without thereby ceasing to be human, so too our human nature is called to an intimate union with the divine nature; we are created, that we may be deified in Christ. And so the icon is at once a revelation of God made man, and of all of us made god in Him. In it, we see how the *kenosis* of the eternal Son—His self-outpouring in the poverty and frailty of infancy, manhood, weariness, sorrow, suffering and death — is also simultaneously our *plerosis* — the filling of our nature with the imperishable splendor of divine beauty and limitless life, the light of rebirth and of resurrection.

In a very profound sense, the entire life of the Christian should be an ascent of Mount Tabor, a penitent yet joyous approach to the Christ who is Himself the Temple of the Glory, from whom the *Shekinah* that resided in the Holy of Holies is now shed forth upon all of creation, and into whose presence we are now able to enter without being slain. The icon of the Transfiguration should draw us into an ever deeper contemplation of who Christ is, what light comes with Him into the world, how we are to see and be seen in that light, and how we are to be changed by it. To gaze at the icon in the correct attitude of devotion, and momentarily removed from all profane concerns, is to acquire the proper orientation of our vision, thought, desire, and will: the face of God, the splendor of the Kingdom, the divine destiny that is the vocation of the living soul. The icon of the Transfiguration is one visible aspect of an infinite summons, calling us to a God of inexhaustible goodness, in whom we always live, move, and have our being, and into whom we are meant to venture forever, into an ever greater embrace of His beauty, passing from glory to glory, eternally.

In a sense, every iconographer is always engaged, in some sense, in depicting the Transfiguration, no matter which image he or she is "writing."

Byzantine iconography, as scarcely needs be said, is an extraordinarily stylized form of art, and this is so for a very particular reason: the figures of the icon are not meant to be seen in a natural light, or even in natural perspective. They are, rather, images in which we see the events and persons of scripture and of ecclesial history as, on the one hand, concrete and earthly and, on the other, ethereal and heavenly. The icon is—at least, according to the piety of the Eastern Christian world—a window upon eternity, mediating between the present and the Kingdom that is to come. And, through this window, not only do we look from this world into the Kingdom; our gaze is met by the eyes of another, who looks out from the Kingdom and holds us in his or her gaze in turn (for every icon, according to the theology of the East, is somehow a true "face" of the person it portrays). Every icon, therefore, is already a transfiguration, a dreamlike marriage between the terrestrial and the celestial, and between the temporal and the eternal. The Transfiguration icon itself, therefore, is in a sense the most "transparent" of icons—even, one might suggest, the icon *par excellence.*

Solrunn Nes is an ideal guide to the iconography of the Transfiguration, in all its dimensions: technical, historical, theological, and aesthetic. She is far more than merely a scholar of the relevant material. She is one of the most accomplished iconographers in the world today; and the icons she produces have few modern rivals, for beauty or for refinement of technique. Her work is, in every significant sense, thoroughly traditional and thoroughly original. Without departing from the canonical rules of Eastern iconography, or from the traditional forms long established for the depiction of Christ and His saints, she nevertheless imbues her work with an extraordinary quality of line and coloration that is entirely her own, and that at times achieves an almost mesmerizing loveliness. (Something of her gifts can be seen—at least, insofar as photographic reproduction allows—in her *The Mystical Language of Icons,* also published by Eerdmans). This makes *The Uncreated Light* more, then, than a simple study. Solrunn Nes being herself someone who enjoys a rare and privileged insight into the "art of transfiguration," so to speak, her book possesses an authority and a completeness of perspective that place it in a very exclusive category. The appearance of this book, in its present edition, is an occasion for rejoicing.

DAVID BENTLEY HART

PREFACE

The Uncreated Light: An Iconographical Study of the Transfiguration in the Eastern Church is a book at the crossroads of theology and art. In accordance with the structure of the narrative in the Gospel of the Transfiguration of Jesus, the book is divided into three main parts. The first part consists of a presentation of the iconographical theme, exemplified by four representative works of art dating from the mid-sixth to the fifteenth centuries. The descriptive part is designed to correspond with Christ's ascent "up into a high mountain"; and through a thorough analysis of the pictorial language of the art works it provides the necessary preludium to the penetration, in the second part of the book, into the meaning and significance of the Transfiguration as an historical event.

Central to this event is the vision of light, the self-revelation of God through a manifestation of the Uncreated Light. In a general discussion based on a wise selection of art works and texts the reader is led into Orthodox interpretation of the event and to an ever widening understanding of the meaning of the Theophany on the mountain. The discussion leads from Bethlehem to Tabor.

The fundamental importance of the Incarnation within the religion is unfolded, not only in relation to the Transfiguration, but also in regard to essential manifestations of Orthodox teaching and belief, such as the concept of deification (theosis) of the believer and the very praxis of icon painting. In succinct fashion, the theological and dogmatical, religious and eschatological, anthropological and cosmological implications of the Transfiguration as an

xvi

Preface

historical and iconographical theme are elucidated from ever changing view-points, with reference to well-chosen art works (like paintings by Theophane the Greek and Rublev) and to liturgical and patristic texts ranging from the Apostolical period and up to the middle of the fourteenth century.

At this point Gregory Palamas stands forth as the protagonist: the interpretation of the iconographical and the pictorial properties of the Transfiguration culminates in the presentation of the light mysticism of the monastic Hesychast movement. Fundamental to Hesychasm is the theophany of the uncreated light on the mountain, interpreted as God's uncreated energy. When this immaterial light-energy illuminates and makes translucent the body of deified man, it takes place in a continuation of the Theophany on Tabor. Guides in the meandering into the lofty spheres of orthodox mysticism are the modern orthodox theologians Vladimir Lossky, John Meyendorff and Kallistos Ware.

In the third and last part of the book, the reader is brought down from the high mountain and back to the starting point. By means of the deeper knowledge of the multifaceted meaning of the Transfiguration won on "the mountain," the images analyzed in the opening sections are made the object of concluding, comprehensive exegesis.

Solrunn Nes studied icon painting in Finland with Robert de Caluwé (1983), and in Athens, at the Academy of Fine Arts (1985). She has travelled extensively in Greece, Turkey, the former Yugoslavia, Russia and Egypt. This book was originally presented — in Norwegian — as a thesis for her master's degree in Art History, at the University of Bergen (1992). The Norwegian version was published in 1995 as *Det Uskapte Lyset*.

Solrunn Nes combines theological knowledge and religious feeling with art historical proficiency and the theoretical and practical command of icon painting. *The Uncreated Light* is a well-written and agreeable book; stimulating and well informed. It bears witness to the author's artistic competence, as well as to a deep, intellectual and spiritual comprehension of Orthodox art based on her dual activity as an artist and an art historian, and a warm sympathy with this art as an expression of faith.

The art historian, like the theologian, the specialist, like the general reader, will benefit greatly from the reading of this book.

Bergen, July 15, 1998   HJALMAR TORP

INTRODUCTION

Within the abundant iconographical tradition of the Eastern Church, the Transfiguration of Jesus Christ is a subject which has an especially rich content. The purpose of studying this theme is to achieve a greater insight into the connection between an iconographical representation and theological interpretation.

The structure of this thesis is inspired by the biblical narrative itself, which has three parts. The story begins with an ascent — "anabasis": Jesus went up to a high mountain together with his three closest disciples — Peter, James and John. While there, they were enveloped in a transcendent light allowing them to partake of a divine vision. They were witnesses of the self-revelation of God — a "theophany." After the experience they descended from the mountain — "katabasis." The disciples were left with an impression which coloured everything they were to encounter. This epical structure of the Transfiguration theme is also the model of how this theme is understood.

I. The Ascent

The first part of this thesis corresponds with *the ascent* and includes a presentation of the iconographical material — in other words — the purely pictorial elements. Here we will look closely at four variations of the Transfiguration made over a period of nine hundred years, which represent very different ways of depicting the subject. We will begin with two Byzantine apse mosaics from the mid-sixth century, followed by an Ottonian manuscript illumination from the eleventh century and, lastly, a Russian icon thought to be from the fifteenth century. The analysis of each work includes a description, a formal analysis and an identification. Knowledge of the pictorial language provides a basis for understanding the inner meaning of the event. This "ascent" will prepare us for what we will see in the next chapter.

II. The Vision of Light

In this phase, which according to our metaphor represents the actual *vision of light,* we will explore the many-faceted theological interpretation of the Transfiguration of Jesus. This incident in the life of Jesus has been a source of inspiration for a comprehensive patristic literature which contemplated the essential qualities of God, mankind and creation and their intrinsic relationship. Our imaginary stay on the mountaintop will therefore initiate a discussion of the theological, anthropological and cosmological implications of the Transfiguration. Such a rough outline naturally demands many subpoints. For this reason, its dogmatical, sacramental, liturgical, didactical and eschatological aspects will be brought under the microscope.

As a concrete point of departure, we will start with our four motifs. Despite this pictorial material offering different versions of the subject, it is not meant to be a comprehensive interpretation. Rather, we have chosen to show what is most pertinent to each work. The goal of this selective approach is to achieve a deeper understanding of the different facets of this complex motif.

As we progress, we will show the contours of a unique spirituality which has its most concentrated and ideal expression in the Transfiguration. This spiritual direction is known as "Orthodox light mysticism" or "Hesychasm" and derives from the Greek word "hesychia," which implies rest, that of being still. Those who practiced and defended hesychasm viewed the Transfiguration as the model and aim for their contemplative life.

In order to acquaint ourselves with this system of thought we will make

a thematic cross section through a selection of relevant sources. This literature was written from the time of the apostles up to the middle of the fourteenth century and includes commentaries, bible texts, quotes from the
desert fathers, homilies on the Transfiguration, excerpts from monastic and
apologetic literature together with conciliar, liturgical and dogmatic texts.

In-depth commentaries and information which can put these sources
into an appropriate ecclesiastical and historical context are written by three
contemporary Orthodox theologians: Vladimir Lossky, John Meyendorff
and Kallistos Ware, and build mainly on the understanding of mystical theology.

III. The Descent

The last part of the book is a parallel to *the descent* and is a phase where the
insight we receive in the main section of the book is applied to the iconographical material presented in chapter one. By comparing the art works we
can more easily obtain an understanding of the similarities and differences
in the iconographical and theological emphases of each work. Here we will
gather the threads of the constituent motifs into a concluding summary.

We will also look at how theology casts light on the changes which
occurred in the representation of the Transfiguration throughout the first
millennium. Is there a connection between the theological and the iconographical development? Do the written texts provide a reason for representing the motif in a new way, or is the motif the same, but understood differently in accordance with the new questions posed by theology? In other
words, is it the motif of the Transfiguration or the understanding of it
which has changed? We shall seek answers to these and similar questions in
this last part of the book.

Chapter I

THE ASCENT

Byzantine Monumental Mosaic, Sinai (565)

Description

In the Greek Orthodox monastery on the southern point of the Sinai peninsula, oral tradition has it that Moses saw the burning bush — at the foot of Mount Sinai.[1] The fortress and monastery were built during the rule of Justinian I the Great (527-565) and the inscriptions on the roof beams indicate that the building took place between 548 and 565.[2] The monastery which Justinian dedicated to Mary, the Mother of God, was later dedicated to Saint Catherine of Alexandria, a martyr from the early fourth century.

The original decoration of the basilica is a monumental mosaic, dated about 565-566,[3] and fills the upper part of the apse. It is divided into three sections, stacked one over the other. The lowest and largest section has a spacious position in the apsidal vault, while the two other mosaics cover the wall area of the triumphal arch in front of the apse. In a sense they encircle and crown the main motif.

---

1. Kurt Weitzmann, *Studies in the Arts of Sinai,* p. 5.
2. Georg H. Forsyth and Kurt Weitzmann, *The Monastery of Saint Catherine of Mount Sinai, The Church and Fortress of Justinian,* p. 11.
3. Gertrud Schiller, *Ikonographie der christlicher Kunst I,* p. 156.

I

The Apse

The mosaic in the apse is remarkable for its monumentality and acts as the leading motif not only because of its size, but also for its placement and composition (plate 1). The whole scene is framed by a wide, dark blue band with 32 medallions. Except for a Greek cross in the middle, all the medallions are portaits of men. In the middle of the scene we see a majestic man in full frontality. His right hand is held up in front of his chest while his left hand is covered by his cloak. His countenance with large, widely opened eyes is framed by long dark hair and a beard. Around his head shines a halo with an inscribed cross. His whole figure stands against the background of an elliptical mandorla made in varied blue tones. Eight beams of light project out from the mandorla. Five of these point to each of the five men who either stand, kneel or lie in a half circle around the central figure. He receives their gaze while they gesture back to him. There are no other compositional elements.

The Triumphal Arch

The uppermost section of the arch shows two scenes divided from each other by two niche-shaped windows. To the left we see a full-figured man in two thirds profile (plate 5). His back is slightly bent as he works to unloosen his left sandal. He rests his foot on a rock while he turns his face towards a hand which extends from the half circle in the upper right corner of the picture. The man's other sandal is in the lower left corner. In front of him a thick green bush burns brightly and behind his back there is a high cliff. To the right we see an almost mirror image of the same scene except now the man stands upright. Both his hands are covered with his cloak as he stretches out his arms to receive something from the hand in the half circle. He gazes downwards and his feet are bare. Mountains loom to the right and the left.

Two flying angels dominate the middle picture plane and form a mirror image of each other. They stretch towards the central medallion in the apex of the arch in which there is a depiction of a lamb. Their forward-reaching hands hold a sphere inscribed with a cross. In the other hand they hold a long staff surmounted by a cross. Under the angels, on each side of the arch, we find two other medallions; the left one contains a man's head and the right, a woman's.

Formal Analysis

Composition

The composition of this entire mosaic is carefully designed to fit the architectural form of the apse in such a way that picture and building are fully integrated. Symmetry and a strong central axis pervade the composition and create balance and weight. Each picture plane is framed by a geometrically constructed scheme. The forms which are repeated are the square, triangle, circle and semicircle.

If we ignore all the faces in the medallions, we see that the centrally placed man in the mandorla is the only one that fully faces us. Each pictorial element outside of the vertical mid axis has a balancing element on the other side. The balance lies here in the magnetic field between the figures. The man in the mandorla is the only figure who is intrinsically balanced, thus providing a natural focus about which the other figures find their orientation.

Depth and Perspective

The two upper pictures have a kind of mountainous landscape. The man has rocky ground under his feet but it is not so barren that a few plants cannot grow. In the picture on the left we see two clear examples of overlapping; the bent knee which hides the man's left forearm and the mountain rising from behind his back (plate 5). If we look closer, however, we notice that the mountain does not extend down to the ground level as we would, logically, expect. Gold fills the space linking the figure with the border — probably in order to distinguish the outline of the man's clothing. This illogicality indicates that it was more important to create an easily recognizable scene than a correct rendition of all the details.

The only formal elements which create space in the picture are the examples of overlapping, together with the light and shadow on the clothing and mountains. We find no lines of perspective which give depth. The picture on the right is even more two-dimensional in comparison (plate 6). Here each pictorial element is isolated so that we get a row of forms; mountain — man — mountain, without any kind of overlapping.

The angels have no such stages. They appear as if they sway freely against the golden background and thus avoid appearing as though they are in a room. The impression we might have of depth arises from the way their drapery is modelled. Here we sometimes notice dramatic transitions between dark and light according to how deep the folds are. This is naturally also the case with all the other drapery, but here it is most apparent.

The group of figures in the apse have already received a physical room which is the apse itself. The concave curving makes the outer figures stand directly across from each other. They exist both in the plane and in the concrete architectural room. This is a quality a flat picture can never have. The surroundings consist merely of a mandorla, eight beams of light and a long, narrow strip of ground on which the men are placed, while the central figure stands firmly in the mandorla without any visible ground. The law of gravity appears not to apply for him. The two kneeling men create a sense of depth in that their legs point diagonally into the room. The even gold background both here and elsewhere contributes to the picture being perceived as flat more than three-dimensional.

Movement

Those figures which are not shown frontally, are seen from a three quarter angle where the upper and lower torsos are slightly twisted. All the figures react in accordance to the pictorial elements ordered along the mid axis. All the action is directed towards the centre.

The man in the uppermost pictorial plane acts in relation to a hand which appears over him. The hand to the left seems inviting and the one on the right giving. The two angels reach towards a lamb while the men in the apse react with animated gestures to the man in the mandorla. The very poses combine dynamics and discipline in such a way that the overriding impression of balance and harmony is not disturbed. The principle is: calm in the middle and action on the periphery.

Colour

The man in the mandorla is a strong focal point both because of his placement, his pose and his intense colouring. He wears a blinding white robe with
light grey-blue shadows in the folds. A gold border decorates parts of his gown
and cloak. The mandorla is divided into four blue fields with the darkest
nearest to the white of the man's gown. The eight beams of light which proceed from the man seem transparent because the colour tone changes —
sometimes lighter, sometimes darker — over the graded blue field. The
clothes of the five men are of weaker pastel colours in a varied range of grey,
brown, violet, blue and green and look like broken reflections of the one
clothed in white. The lower edge of the picture is bordered by bands of yellow,
green and dark green. The wide, dark blue band with the medallion portraits
which frames the picture in the apse, supplements the two purely decorative
borders in gold and green which fill the edge of the triumphal arch. The green
colour is repeated in the angels' wings. They wear grey and white gowns with
flowing blue capes. Blue, white and gold are repeated in the medallions of the
cross and lamb just over the mandorla. The repeated use of colours in all the
scenes facilitates our understanding of their interconnection.

The top pictures are reduced to somber, peaceful nuances of grey,
brown, green and blue. The burning bush in the left scene alone uses red for
more than decorative framing. Otherwise there are no warm colours used
apart from the flesh areas. Because it is the so-called cold colours which
dominate against the flowing background of gold, the mocaic seems to be
both harmonious and intense.

Light

The most immediate impression of light comes from the white-clad man in
the mandorla. He appears as a powerful light source who spreads his abundant light over the five men. Each one is touched by a beam of light and
then indirectly reflects it back. When we observe how the light is used in
the modelling of clothes and faces, we cannot assume any light source coming from outside the picture. The light comes from different sources — as if
each figure stood isolated. No figure is emphasized more than any other by
way of external lighting.

It is first and foremost the gold which indicates that light comes primarily from within the picture itself. Because this metal has the unique ability to reflect light, it is especially well suited for creating an impression of the picture showing light emanating from within. (This phenomenon is called "sent light.") The use of gold where one could expect a sky blue colour, signalizes that the episodes they depict did not necessarily take place on earth. The lack of cast shadows is another indicator that the laws of nature do not apply here. We are witness to unique scenes which transcend the normal realm of human experience.

Today's furnishing in the monastery renders the mosaics barely visible from the nave. The original dialogue between the main body of the building, the decoration and the liturgy is disturbed by a high iconostasis — a wall of icons — which blocks the view into the choir. This iconostasis was built in the eighteenth century because of new liturgical practice. Thus the apse mosaics were left with a minor role to play. Windows in the nave allow for only partial light to seep into the apse. Since the viewer must walk behind the iconostasis to see the mosaic, there is neither enough light nor distance to survey it properly.

Identification

The presupposition for gathering information on the picture from sources outside of the work itself, is naturally the basic knowledge about the people who planned, built and used the building and designed its decoration. This frame of reference is widely understood as the Judeo-Christian cultural heritage which developed within the Byzantine world of the sixth century. Relevant written sources would therefore be the Old and New Testaments along with texts from the early church tradition.

The Apse

The mosaic in the apse is adorned with Greek inscriptions naming each person represented — except for the man in the mandorla. This helps us to identify each individual, but in order to confirm which episode it illustrates we must resort to external sources — in this case texts from the synoptic gospels — Matthew, Mark and Luke along with the second epistle of Peter. Here we find the stories which give the basis for the iconographical representation.

The gospels tell that Jesus took his three closest disciples, Peter, James and John, up to a high mountain. While there Jesus was changed into a being of light. Both his face and clothing changed their appearance. Matthew writes that "his face did shine as the sun, and his raiment was white as the light" (Matt. 17:2). Mark compares the shining clothing to the common practice of whitening cloth by bleaching it in the sun, as "no fuller on earth can white them" (Mark 9:3). Luke describes how this transformation happened during prayer: "And as he prayed, the fashion of his countenance was altered, and his raiment was white and glistening" (Luke 9:29).

After the transfiguration of Jesus the disciples witnessed the Old Testament prophets Moses and Elijah in conversation with Jesus. Only Luke mentions the content of the conversation being the fate of Jesus in Jerusalem and that the disciples then fell into a deep sleep. All the gospels tell that Peter, in a state of fear and confusion, suggested building tents for each of the shining people.

The disciples were even more afraid when they were enveloped in a radiant cloud and heard a voice from it say: "This is my beloved Son, in whom I am well pleased; hear ye him" (Matt. 17:5). The account in Matthew is clearest in describing the disciples' reaction of fear when he writes that "they fell on their face, and were sore afraid" (Matt. 17:6). After the vision is over and Jesus is alone with the disciples, he comforts them saying: "Arise, and be not afraid" (Matt. 17:7).

It is thus that the three gospel writers present the episode which is called the transfiguration of Jesus. Peter defends himself against those who suspect that the experience was only a made-up story when he in his letter emphasizes that he and the other two disciples were eyewitnesses to that which happened and that they really heard a voice which spoke: "from the excellent glory" (II Peter 1:16-18).

The Latin word "transfiguratio" can be translated by "to be changed into another form" or "being changed into a glorified state," while the Greek word "metamorphosis" means "to go from one state of being to another."

The texts say nothing specific about where the Transfiguration took place geographically, just that it happened on "a high mountain." It was Cyril of Jerusalem (ca. 315-386) who confirmed that it was the holy mountain Tabor in Galilee. Since then this location has been the generally accepted one.[4]

The Triumphal Arch

The three pictures on the triumphal arch have no inscriptions that can be easily identified. There we are dependent on recognizing the scene based upon other sources. Because of knowledge of the Old Testament story about how God revealed himself for Moses, we can confirm that the left scene represents Moses' first meeting with God in the form of a thorn bush burning without being consumed.

> Moses was looking after the flock of Jethro, his father-in-law, priest of Midian. He led his flock to the far side of the wilderness and came to Horeb, the mountain of God. There the angel of Yahweh appeared to him in the shape of a flame of fire, coming from the middle of the bush. Moses looked; there was the bush blazing but it was not being burnt up. "I must go and look at this strange sight," Moses said, "and see why the bush is not burnt." Now Yahweh saw him go forward to look, and God called to him from the middle of the bush. "Moses, Moses!" he said. "Here I am," he answered. "Come no nearer," he said. "Take off your shoes, for the place on which you stand is holy ground. I am the God of your father," he said, "the God of Abraham, the God of Isaac and the God of Jacob." At this Moses covered his face, afraid to look at God. (Exod. 3:1-6)

Horeb is another name for Mount Sinai. It was at the base of this mountain that Moses saw the burning bush and it was here Justinian chose to build the monastery which would underline the connection between central theophanies in the Old and New Testaments as explained by the Church. By choosing such a "locus sanctus" the spiritual continuity was assured as well as providing it with a natural authority and prestige.

---

4. Gertrud Schiller, *Ikonographie der christlicher Kunst I,* p. 155.

In the picture on the right we see that Moses receives the law from "the hand of God." This episode occurred on Mount Sinai.

Yahweh said to Moses, "Come up to me on the mountain and stay there while I give you the stone tablets — the law and the commandments — that I have written for their instruction." (. . .) And Moses went up the mountain. The cloud covered the mountain, and the glory of Yahweh settled on the mountain of Sinai; for six days the cloud covered it, and on the seventh day Yahweh called to Moses from inside the cloud. To the eyes of the sons of Israel the glory of Yahweh seemed like a devouring fire on the mountain top. Moses went right into the cloud. He went up the mountain, and stayed there for forty days and forty nights. (. . .) When he had finished speaking with Moses on the mountain of Sinai, he gave him the two tables of Testimony, tables of stone inscribed by the finger of God. (Exod. 24:12, 15-18; 31:18)

Moses broke the stone tablets when he saw that the children of Israel had begun to worship idols while he was away. The covenant had to be renewed when he came down from the mountain.

When comparing the texts about the transfiguration of Jesus and Moses receiving the ten commandments, one finds several noticeable parallels. Both experiences took place on a high mountain. Moses went up to Mount Sinai alone. Only the three closest disciples of Jesus went with him up to Mount Tabor. On Mount Sinai God's glory was revealed in the form of a blazing fire. On Mount Tabor the disciples were overwhelmed by an intense light. Both Moses and the disciples were enveloped in a cloud. Both times the voice of God was heard. It was told of Moses that his face shone because the Lord had spoken to him (Exod. 34:29). Likewise the face of Jesus was changed when he was transfigured. "And his face did shine as the sun," wrote Matthew (Matt. 17:2).

The pictorial plane between the Moses motifs and the Transfiguration does not take its iconography from any particular biblical text. Both the compositional and thematic centre is a lamb in a medallion above the apex of the triumphal arch. John the Baptist is the first to point to Jesus as God's pascal lamb when he says: "Behold the lamb of God, which taketh away the

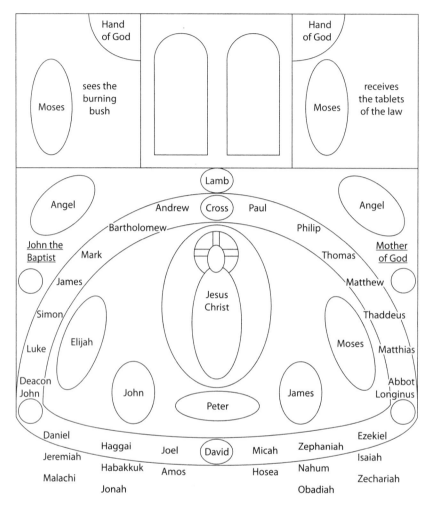

This model shows the identification of people, groups and single elements in the mosaic in the monastery of Saint Catherine.

sin of the world" (John 1:29). Paul uses the same metaphor when he explains the death of Jesus in light of the old Jewish sacrificial practice instituted by Moses: "For even Christ our passover is sacrificed for us" (I Cor. 5:7). The same theme is repeated in the eschatological visions in John's Revelation:

> Then I saw, standing between the throne with its four animals and the circle of the elders, a lamb that seemed to have been sacrificed; In

> my vision, I heard the sound of an immense number of angels gathered round the throne and the animals and the elders; there were ten thousand times ten thousand of them and thousands upon thousands, shouting, "The lamb that was sacrificed is worthy to be given power, riches, wisdom, strength, honour, glory and blessing." (Rev. 5:6, 11)

In this motif "the host of angels" is reduced to two who represent the heavenly host worshipping the lamb. They lift up the kingly attributes — the sceptre and the orb — both decorated with a cross. The cross is also visible behind the lamb showing its paradoxical character as both a symbol for suffering and victory.

Directly below each angel there is a medallion, with a man's head to the left and a woman's head to the right. Here we see an early example of a pictorial representation which would later become a convention of the Byzantine iconography, namely the deesis-group. "Deesis" is a Greek word for intercession. The simplest version includes the enthroned Christ with John the Baptist to the left and Mary, the Mother of God, to the right, both turned to Christ with their hands lifted in prayer. In this case the scene is reduced to three pictographical medallions. On the basis of this information the scenes can be identified as the worship of the lamb in heaven — in other words, an expression of the heavenly liturgy — or perhaps a compressed representation of the final judgement where John the Baptist and Mary the Mother of God are regarded as central figures whose function is to pray on behalf of sinners.

Byzantine Monumental Mosaic, Ravenna (549)

Description

The basilica Sant Apollinare in Classe in Ravenna was founded and begun during the office of Bishop Ursicinus (532-536) and consecrated by Bishop Maximilian in 549. The architect was Julianus Argentarius,[5] and as with the monastery in the Sinai desert, so also this monumental building was erected during the reign of Emperor Justinian.

The mosaics in the apse are from different periods. The main motif in the apse, the four figures between the windows, the two palms and the two archangels on either side of the triumphal arch are all part of the original decoration. The two mosaics to the right and left of the apse windows are from the latter half of the seventh century while the two areas above the triumphal arch probably were added during the ninth century. Here the dat-

---

5. Otto G. von Simson, *Sacred Fortress, Byzantine Art and Statecraft in Ravenna,* pp. 5-6 and 10.

ing varies somewhat. At the bottom of each side of the arch we see two men in half-figure. These have been dated about the year 1000.[6]

The later works which will not have a decisive role in our research, will be presented and identified along with the original mosaics. These will be identified after they are described and given a formal analysis.

The Apse

On entering the basilica, our attention is immediately drawn towards the large mosaic which fills the apse vault (plate 7). We look into a celestial landscape where all is graceful and harmonious. In the middle of this landscape a formally vested man stands in a frontal pose (plate 8). He rests most of his weight on his left foot and raises his arms, the palms of his hands being open. He wears a white, foot-length alba and a brownish chasuble speckled with gold. Over his shoulders hangs a white stole. He has short grey hair and a beard. His face has mild, even features and he gazes at us with large, brown eyes.

Along the lower border twelve white lambs walk towards the man — six from either side. Between each of them there is a bush of white lilies and between their hooves there are two small flowering plants. These pictorial elements emphasize the consistent rhythm permeating the entire composition. The green part of the picture is covered with small, hilly forms, bushes, trees and birds spread evenly about. The only break in the symmetry is the three lambs further up in the picture — one on the left and two to the right of the circular disc which dominates the middle field. Against a sky blue star-strewn background there is a gold Latin cross decorated with precious stones. A man's head is placed in the centre of the cross. The three lambs lift their heads and look towards the circle.

In the upper part of the picture — over the landscape and around the top of the circle — there are three elements appearing out of the cloudy gold background — two white-clad men in half-figure and a hand. The two men float on the clouds above the tree tops and stop on each side of the circle while the hand reaches down from the arches. Both of the men and the hand point in the direction of the cross.

---

6. These dates are based on the presentation of Sant Apollinare in Classe given by Giuseppe Bovini in *Ravenna Mosaics* (Oxford, 1978), p. 49.

Just under the mosaic there are five niche-shaped windows. The walls between the windows make four pictorial planes which also have the illusion of being niches such that the whole arrangement looks like a colonnade. In each of these niches stands a frontally posed man with a bejeweled book in his left hand. Their right hands are placed on their chests. Gold crowns hover above their heads and their clothes are similar to those worn by the centrally placed man above.

The Triumphal Arch

Even though it is the large apse mosaic which is of primary interest to us in this context, we will also describe the other pictures which surround it.

In the top mid section of the triumphal arch we see a frontally viewed man in half-figure inscribed in a round medallion. He holds a book to his chest with his left arm while lifting his right hand in a sign of blessing. There is a cross in his halo. We are looking at a conventional representation of Christ Pantocrator — the Ruler of all. He is flanked by four winged beings, each holding a book — to the left we can recognize an eagle and a person, on the right side there is a lion and an ox — as mentioned in the same order — these represent the gospel writers John, Matthew, Mark and Luke. The space between the figures is filled with horizontal cloud forms in different nuances of pink and light blue, while the background is dark blue.

In the section immediately below this and surmounting the apex of the triumphal arch we see a similar distribution of pale clouds, this time on a gold ground. From both sides there are six white lambs coming out of city gates. They walk on light green turf which naturally follows the ascending line of the triumphal arch. They walk as though in a ceremonial procession towards the centrally placed Christ figure above them.

Just under the city gates there are two date palms standing against a dark blue background. They bend slightly inward and thus elegantly fill the triangular form in which they are inscribed. Under the palms there are two archangels — Michael stands to the left and Gabriel to the right. They are clothed in formal aristocratic garments and each holds a banner with the Greek inscription "agios, agios, agios," which means "holy, holy, holy." The background has again changed into gold. They stand on golden footstools in a green landscape with flowers in the foreground. The lowest mosaics show the busts of two men and, as mentioned earlier, were made at a much later date.

Later Additions to the Apse

The two remaining pictures to the right and left of the windows are not clearly visible in plate 7. On the left is a representation of Emperor Constantine IV and his brothers Heraclius and Tiberius together with the archbishops Maurus and Reparatus. The latter was bishop of Ravenna from 673 to 679 and became wealthy through his association with the emperor. He managed to achieve Ravenna's independence from the church in Rome. This mosaic is heavily restored.

On the right is a group of four people standing in a semi-circle around a table. Behind is an older man standing in a frontal position. A broach pins together his golden-edged cape and his long, grey hair is crowned with a diadem. The young man to the left is clothed in fringed leather and a loose cloak is draped over his shoulders. In his outstretched hands he holds a lamb over the table. On the other side there is another elderly man with a boy in front of him. A hand emerges from some small clouds and points down to the table on which there is a carafe and two round items with a cross in the centre. The picture is framed by two decorated pillars and a curtain which hangs down on each side.

This is a concentrated motif which symbolizes the sacrifice of Abel, Melchizedek and Abraham. The theme here is recognizable from San Vitale, another church in Ravenna, but here the three scenes are condensed into one.

Formal Analysis

Composition

The composition is organized by strict symmetry. The various pictorial elements are placed against a background built up by simple geometric forms — in particular the rectangle, the circle and the triangle. The craftsmen have utilized the structure of the architecture itself in the composition by allowing the figures and pictorial elements to reflect these fundamental geometric forms. The gently curving palms echoing the line of the triumphal arch fill their allotted space with long, slender trunks and a fan-shaped crown. The twelve lambs along the lower picture plane emphasize and give weight to the horizontal axis, while the two rows of lambs converging over the triumphal arch mark an ascent which is the natural quality of that pictorial plane.

The four individual elements placed centrally in vertically ascending order are: the full-figured man, the cross with a man's head in the centre of the medallion, the hand coming out of the cloud and the medallion with a man's bust — these make up a mid axis to which the other pictorial elements are subordinated. As we see, frontality is reserved for the figures along this axis. All the lambs are shown in profile and the two men in half-figure are seen in three quarter profile.

Depth and Perspective

The most important indication of depth in this pictorial program is the actual construction of the apse itself. It is like "a room within a room." The pictorial plane in the apse is not "flat," but follows the concave curve of the half circle. This gives the effect of the heavens actually forming a vault over the landscape. Since there are no perspective lines that can be used to give the illusion of depth, we cannot decide if we are looking at a hill or a flat field.

Each individual form has a strong outline and stands isolated and clearly distinct against the background. No one thing is emphasized more than any other. The only example of overlapping is the two lambs to the right of the circle. The distance between the pictorial elements does not indicate that any elements are further away. An exception to this rule seems to be the face in the cross which is smaller than the faces of the three other men. Because the medallion creates its own separate picture, one cannot compare it with the other forms but must therefore evaluate it separately.

The different pictorial elements on the green ground are ordered in tiered groups along horizontal lines. The lowest tier consists of lambs converging in single file on the centrally placed man, above which stretches a slightly uneven border of rocks and plants. Over this is a wider border of rocks, small flowers, birds and bushes and uppermost are found three large trees, possibly cypress, and three lambs. The many rocks or outcroppings are interspersed between the bushes and trees which are viewed slightly from above, while the rest of the composition is seen directly from the front. This indicates that the craftsmen have used an inconsistent perspective, but this is not overly noticeable.

In this analysis of depth and perspective, it is natural to say that the elements are placed over, under and to the side of each other rather than in front or behind. The reason for this is that we are dealing with a landscape that has been folded out and flattened. There are, so to speak, no indicators which give the illusion of its being three-dimensional.

The two archangels that flank the large apse mosaic stand on a rectangular step which at a closer look tapers downwards in the picture. The step is seen from a high vantage point and is narrower in the front than at the back. The converging lines do not meet in a vanishing point as we would expect from a logically constructed room, but lead our eyes towards an infinite room which breaks out of the frame of the physical picture. By following the converging lines in the other direction, we discover that the vanishing point ends up with us as viewers. This reversed perspective entails the change of our role from being viewers into being viewed. The picture draws us and makes us participants in a dialogue where we are no longer the sovereign subject.

Movement

The expression of static calm is emphasized by the pervading strong symmetry. All pictorial elements along the vertical mid axis are frontally viewed and there is also a regular horizontal repetition of forms. The movement seems frozen even though one or two birds flap their wings.

In spite of the formal pose we can perceive a certain degree of interaction between the figures. Horizontally the action is divided into two fields: at the bottom the man standing in the middle of the row of lambs, on the top the medallion surrounded by a hand, two men in half-figure and three lambs. The men turn towards the medallion with pointing hands, the lambs lift their heads and look up. It is the seemingly static figures along the vertical axis which begin the movement and cause the other figures to react.

Colour

The colours which make up the background for the three largest picture planes in the central axis mosaic are green, blue and gold. This dispersion of colour gives the picture a light and airy impression, bordering on cold. There are many variations of green which dominate both in intensity and their expanse. The bright, white lambs are a marked contribution because they are so noticeable against the green background. White is also used on the clothing where its effect is more subtle. Brown is repeated often — on the stones, the three trunks and the central man's clothing. What we traditionally call warm colours — red and yellow — are used on less important details like birds and flowers and in the decorative borders around the different pictures.

Light

Daylight comes into the basilica through a row of niche-shaped windows along the walls of the side aisles and along the upper wall of the main nave. In addition there are five windows in the apse itself. This natural light streaming into the church is sufficient for viewing the mosaics during the day. Before electricity was introduced, it was common to light up a church with torches when it was dark outside. The mosaic tesserae are pressed into the mortar in such a way that light is reflected at different angles. The living light from the torches made the mosaics seem to vibrate in a way that artificial or electrical lighting cannot reproduce.

If we ignore the external lighting factors and concentrate on how light is used within the mosaic itself, we can confirm that no area or part of the composition is more accentuated than any other. The entire surface appears in an evenly diffused light that does not come from a definable source. It is rather a *universal light* that is omnipresent. There are therefore no sharply outlined shadows and we must search for a light source elsewhere, namely in the picture itself. The gold is understood as *sent light* and has been previously discussed in connection with the Sinai mosaics. The same principle also applies here.

Identification

The Apse

The four men represented on the walls between the windows in the apse can be identified on the basis of Latin inscriptions. Reading from the left to the right we see the bishops Ecclesius (521-32), Severus (340), Ursus (398-424?) and Ursicinus (532-36). The dates refer to the duration of their time as bishops of Ravenna. Severus was the first bishop who can be firmly documented. Ursicinus was bishop when the basilica was in the process of being built.

Now we will direct our attention to the mosaic in the cupola of the apse and begin with the medallion. At each end of the arms of the cross we find abbreviated inscriptions. On the top we can read the Greek word ICQUS, which reads "fish," but which in the early Christian era was used as a code for "Jesus Christ, Son of God, Saviour." On the horizontal cross arms stand the letters A and W, the first and last letters of the Greek alphabet. They allude to two texts in the Revelation of Saint John:

"I am the Alpha and the Omega," says the Lord God, who is, who was, and who is to come, the Almighty. (Rev. 1:8)

I am the Alpha and the Omega, the first and the Last, the Beginning and the End. (Rev. 22:13)

Under the foot of the cross we find the Latin inscription "Salus Mundi," meaning "Salvation of the World." Christ, whose face is represented in the middle of the cross, can thus be identified not only by his portrait and the inscription, but by the cross — his most well known sign. The medallion is flanked by two men in half-figure who are named in Latin — Moses to the left and Elijah to the right.

The tall man beneath the medallion is identified as Saint Apollinaris. His halo and uplifted hands indicate that he is a saint in prayer. According to the biographical legend called "Passio Sancti Apollinaris," he was said to have been the first missionary and bishop of Ravenna, ordained and sent by the apostle Peter. By dating the christianization of Ravenna to the apostolic age, the writer aimed at raising the city's status, but there is no historical basis for this claim. Excavation of graves indicates that there were Christian congregations in the area from the end of the first century. The basilica Sant Apollinare in Classe was built in close proximity to a Christian grave site from this period.[7]

Thus far the inscriptions have been able to help us. The many lambs in the picture are without a doubt important, but since none of them are individualized in any way, we must count how many there are and how they behave in order to come up with a likely identification. Just under the medallion there are three lambs, one to the left and two to the right. They seem to belong to the scene shown in the upper part of the apse where the medallion is not only the centre of the composition, but also its content. The three lambs are found, in other words, within the same dimension as Moses and Elijah. It is only in the story of the Transfiguration of Jesus that Moses and Elijah are represented simultaneously. Thus the three lambs lose their anonymity and come to represent the three disciples who were witness to the event. Since Peter was the only one who spoke, it is not unreasonable that the creator of the mosaic chose to represent him separated from the others. In which case Peter is on the left and James and John can be seen on the right. The hand appearing over the medallion is a well-known symbol for the invisible God revealing himself. On this occasion God allowed himself to be known through audible speech.

On the lower edge of the picture we see twelve lambs who walk towards Bishop Apollinaris. The number twelve causes one to associate them with the twelve apostles, but the metaphor does not make sense when we look at the motif as a whole. It does not seem logical that Bishop Apollinaris, who himself was a part of the apostolic succession, should be represented as a leader for the first apostles. It is more probable that he is represented as a pastor and intercessor for his flock of believers in Ravenna. The creator of the mosaic has greatly honored Apollinaris by depicting him in the same landscape as the closest disciples of Jesus.

Here it may be relevant to quote Peter Chrysologos (ca. 400-450), who was appointed bishop of Ravenna about the year 435. As the conclusion of a speech in honor of the first bishop of Ravenna, he says:

7. Giuseppe Bovini, *Ravenna* (New York, 1971), p. 9.

The Ascent

Ecce vivit, ecce ut bonus pator suo medio assistit in grege.

Behold, he lives, behold, as a good shepherd he stands amongst his flock.[8]

This quotation is an apt description of how the holy Apollinaris would be represented in a mosaic more than one hundred years later.

The Triumphal Arch

The apostles are found on the triumphal arch represented as two groups of six lambs who walk in a procession up towards the centrally placed Christ Pantocrator in the highest pictorial field. They are shown emerging from two beautifully decorated city gates on either side of the picture. Because of similar motifs in Rome which bear inscriptions, it can be understood that these two gates represent Jerusalem (to the left) and Bethlehem (to the right). A conventional interpretation of this motif says that the lambs going out from Jerusalem symbolize Jewish Christians, while the lambs coming from Bethlehem symbolize Gentile Christians.[9] This scene can therefore be understood as an expression of the universality of the gospel.

As mentioned earlier, the two uppermost pictorial fields of the triumphal arch were made in the eighth or ninth century and cannot be regarded as a part of the original decoration. They are nevertheless clearly intended to complement the main motif in the apse, both in theme and style.

The two smaller fields beneath, with palm trees and archangels, are part of the first pictorial program. Further down on the triumphal arch we see two men in half figure, Matthew to the left and Luke to the right. These mosaics, from the eleventh century, do not blend in with the rest of the decoration both because they are larger in size and because their style is less sophisticated.

8. Ibid., p. 55.
9. Otto G. von Simson, *Sacred Fortress, Byzantine Art and Statecraft in Ravenna*, p. 60.

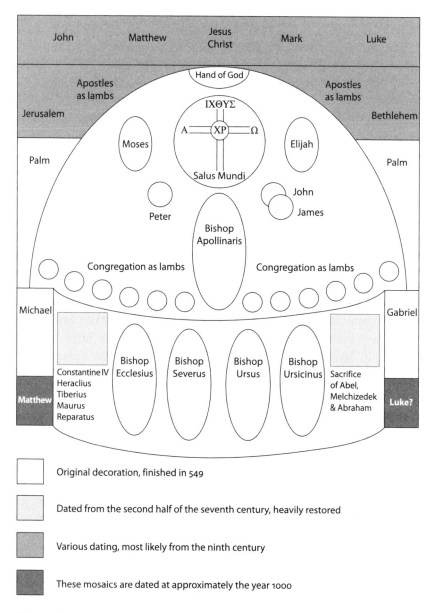

		Jesus		
John	Matthew	Christ	Mark	Luke

Apostles as lambs

Apostles as lambs

Jerusalem

Bethlehem

Hand of God

ΙΧΘΥΣ

A — XP — Ω

Moses

Elijah

Palm

Palm

Salus Mundi

John

Peter

James

Bishop Apollinaris

Congregation as lambs

Congregation as lambs

Michael

Gabriel

Matthew

Constantine IV
Heraclius
Tiberius
Maurus
Reparatus

Bishop Ecclesius

Bishop Severus

Bishop Ursus

Bishop Ursicinus

Sacrifice of Abel, Melchizedek & Abraham

Luke?

Original decoration, finished in 549

Dated from the second half of the seventh century, heavily restored

Various dating, most likely from the ninth century

These mosaics are dated at approximately the year 1000

This model shows the identification of persons, groups and other pictorial elements in the mosaics in Sant Apollinare in Classe together with the dating of different pictorial fields.

Ottonian Manuscript Illumination (Eleventh Century)

Description

The picture we shall now study is taller than it is wide (plate 9). It is divided into four areas such that we have two squares above and two rectangles below. Because of the interaction between the groups of figures, it appears as though the two upper and the two lower sections depict independent pictorial scenes. The division is achieved with the help of thick silver lines, the background is gilded with gold leaf and the entire picture is framed in with a strong reddish brown border.

In the upper left pictorial field we see a swaddled child lying in a crib. The crib is shown with the nearest side being shorter and lower than the one furthest away. The child, who has a golden halo inscribed with a cross, looks up at six winged angels who come dancing and flying down from the frame. By turning the picture upside down, we can more easily see that the angels stand with one foot on the frame while the other is hidden behind it. This gives the impression that they are coming out of a fictive extension of the pictorial frame. Between the child and the angels is a silver star.

In the pictorial field to the right we see a seventh angel who also comes from above. He points towards three eagerly gesticulating men who stand next to a flock of animals. The man closest to the angels points up and turns towards the two others who react with staring expressions and outstretched arms. Some of the animals turn towards the child in the crib and others look towards the men.

The vertical line that divides these two areas is broken by an angel's wing and an animal's snout, giving the impression that the two scenes can be read as one. The horizontal lines, on the other hand, is emphasized by decorative cloud formations which work to bind together the two lower pictorial fields.

The lower left picture shows a rounded mountain in variegated brown tones which occupies almost half of the rectangular area. A tall man in a light blue tunic and gold cape stands in a frontal position on the mountain top. The pictorial elements are organized in such a way that his feet are placed on the ground and his head is in the clouds. His face is young and beardless. He has dark, mid-length hair and his eyes stare intensely. Within the halo a cross is inscribed in silver with blue precious stones. He is flanked by two men who are smaller in scale and stand lower. They turn towards the man in the middle with their face and hands lifted. Both have grey hair and a beard. They are clothed in light green robes and yellow capes which have brown stripes and fringes.

In the lower right pictorial plane we find three men who by their poses and gestures seem to react strongly to what they see on the mountain top. The young man in yellow closest to the mountain breaks the vertical silver line with his foot and falls dramatically backwards. A middle-aged man turns his body away while he looks up at that which seems so frightening. The third and oldest man half stands and half kneels with his hands lifted over his head. These two men have brown and blue clothing. In the area between the three men and the brightly coloured sky formations there are three horizontal silver bands. The middle band contains an inscription in Latin. There is also an inscription on the crib and on the lower border of the frame.

What is striking about these drawings is that the heads, hands and feet are exaggerated in size compared to the rest of the body. This results in very clear and distinct expressions on the faces and in the gestures.

Formal Analysis

Composition

At first glance, the picture can seem unconstructed and confusing. If we let our eye follow the picture sequence as though reading a cartoon series, however, the underlying structure is obvious.

The central compositional principle is, as mentioned before, four picture fields. Together the lines create a Latin cross. If we ignore the vertical line — which is less defined than the horizontal — we find two pictures that naturally belong together both compositionally and thematically. Therefore this analysis will, from this point on, mainly discuss the four scenes as two independent picture fields or compositions. The connection between them will be discussed in more detail later.

In the upper picture both the format and placement of figures work together to emphasize the horizontal dimension. The somewhat unruly row of flying angels corresponds with the child lying in the crib, the animal group and the men. Contact between the angel and the men furthest to the right introduces a diagonal line that binds together these parallel rows.

In the lower picture we find that the three men on the mountain emphasize the vertical dimension. Viewed in isolation, this group is harmoniously complete in terms of symmetry and balance. What disturbs the balance is the group of three men on the right. Despite the distinct separateness of the two groupings we can assume an underlying connection between them. The diagonal line created by the glances of the men up towards the central man on the mountain top parallels the diagonal in the upper picture.

Depth and Perspective

As we already have mentioned, the picture represents two scenes with narrative content. The picture has, in other words, a natural time frame. There is no attempt to contextualize the subject matter spatially but rather the images seem to move both outwards towards the viewer and to recede backwards into another dimension. We can for instance note how the angels' wings, haloes, hands and feet at times extend out of the frame and thus come closer to the viewer. Angels' feet behind the frame or a crib shown in reverse perspective are small indicators that lead our imagination beyond the frame and into a dimension not yet experienced.

In itself the picture plane is first and foremost flat. The plain gold background tends to produce this effect. Landscape and other surroundings which could place the figures in a three-dimensional context are reduced to an absolute minimum. A few examples of overlapping are unable to reduce this fundamental impression of two-dimensionality.

Movement

The picture is permeated by movement. Many figures are depicted with over-animated gestures, twisted bodies, diagonal heads and staring eyes. The clouds billow as in a storm, the ground and mountain have a decorative, undulating form. The garments are painted with quick, almost nervous, but nevertheless controlled brushstrokes.

The only relaxed figures are the child in the crib and the tall man on the mountain just beneath. Restfulness is concentrated on the left side, while the strongest emotional expressions are found on the right. This back-and-forth between passive and active behavior is repeated in both pictures and accounts for the basic action.

The child in the crib and the man on the mountain top are remarkable also because of their larger size in comparison to the other figures. To emphasize individual figures in this way indicates that they have a high rank within a hierachical system. This principle of the most important person being enlarged is known as *hierarchical perspective.*

Colour

The background is covered with gold. The transition between the picture fields along with certain symbolic details is marked with silver. These two precious metals unite the glowing and the cold. They underline the general sense of balanced, yet dynamic colouring. Each field combines the same colours within a limited scale. On the angels' wings and the clouds we find a rhythmic repetition of blue, red and white. In all four pictures there are noticeable elements of reddish brown, ochre and light blue which produce both warmth and light.

Light

The term "manuscript illumination" indicates the fundamental function of light within this particular art form. The manuscript is illuminated — etymologically it means "lighted" by gold and bright colours. The thin parchment is processed calf skin which has the intrinsic quality of translucency. Light is mediated through three materials — the page itself, the gold background and the paint. In addition to this intense "sent light," the highlights on the drapery are placed in such a way that the imagined light sources outside the picture radiate in all directions. It is not a question of any consistent lighting, but rather a light that defies the conventional depiction of space.

Since the pictorial space has such an ambiguous character, the experiences or actions represented can be applicable to all times and places. The picture appears to convey an implicit universality that will have a bearing on the consequent interpretation.

Identification

This manuscript illumination is taken from a copy of the gospels written in Latin where the readings are divided into so-called "pericopes" — a Greek word meaning paragraphs. The texts are organized into a liturgical order which corresponds with the feasts of the church year. The manuscript dates from the end of the eleventh century during the German kingdom at the time of the emperors Otto I, II and III. The illumination can therefore be counted as Ottonian art.

The inscriptions on the page inform us that the picture illustrates the beginning of the gospel of Saint John — the so-called prologue of Saint John.

Et Verbum caro factum est,	The Word was made flesh,
et habitavit in nobis;	he lived among us,
et vidimus gloriam ejus,	and we saw his glory,
gloriam quasi Unigenita a Patre	a glory that is his as the only Son of the Father,
plenum gratiæ et veritatis.	full of grace and truth.

(John 1:14)

In the picture we see an abbreviated version of this quotation written in three lines. The text explains the picture while the picture is an interpretation of the text. The writing "Et Verbum caro factum est" is placed along the inside of the crib where the child lies. In the upper picture we have a pictogram — a summary of the central teaching of the Christian faith — the dogma of the Incarnation. A literal translation of this word is "to put on flesh," in other words, that "God became man in Jesus Christ."

Luke is the evangelist who goes into most depth in describing the historical details of the birth of Jesus. The epical aspects such as angels, shepherds, sheep and the babe in swaddling clothes lying in a manger are from this gospel, while the star is mentioned by Matthew in connection with the story about the wise men.

When we look at the lower motif, we see the words "et habitavit in nobis" written in the open area to the right of the men on the mountain top. Here the transfigured Jesus stands between Moses and Elijah. The inscription is just over the three men who can now be identified as Peter, James and John. The rest of the text has an abbreviated form, almost like a rebus. In this way it can all be fitted onto the bottom line: "*et vidimus gloriam ejus, gloriam quasi Unigenita a Patre plenum gratiæ et veritatis.*"

Since John was the youngest and most visionary of the disciples, it is surely he who is the beardless one closest to the foot of the mountain. He has been thrown to the ground by the overwhelming scene. Peter can be identified by his grey hair and beard. From what we know of these disciples' personalities, we can imagine that John's falling hands express a receptive, contemplative attitude, while the uplifted hands of Peter are a sign that he is active and participative. The more anonymous James seems divided in his reactions. His gaze is rigidly fastened on the altered appearance of the Master. At the same time his body and hands are turned away as if to protect himself from the vision.

Moses and Elijah look almost as though they are mirror images of each other. Their uplifted hands tell that they are involved in a conversation with Jesus, "*of his departure which he was to accomplish in Jerusalem*" (Luke 9:31). The decorative field which emphasizes the division between the upper and lower scenes represents the bright clouds that came and overshadowed them and from which they heard the voice of God.

Within the Orthodox Church John is referred to as John the Theologian because what he writes has a thoroughly reflective character. John gives no story-like discription of the birth of Jesus or of his transfiguration, but the pregnant words that accompany these pictures refer both to the Incarnation and the Transfiguration. These two episodes in the life of Jesus create the clearest historical starting point for the later dogma about the two natures of Jesus.

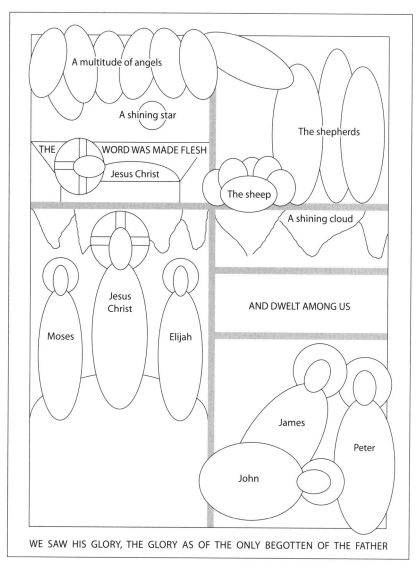

A multitude of angels

A shining star

The shepherds

THE WORD WAS MADE FLESH

Jesus Christ

The sheep

A shining cloud

Jesus Christ

AND DWELT AMONG US

Moses

Elijah

James

Peter

John

WE SAW HIS GLORY, THE GLORY AS OF THE ONLY BEGOTTEN OF THE FATHER

This model shows the identification of persons, groups, individual elements and inscriptions in the Ottonian manuscript illumination.

Russian Transfiguration Icon (1403)

Description

This icon shows a landscape with four caves and three mountain tops (plate 10). The mountains have a diagonal stairlike construction. On the central mountain there stands a white-clad man inside a white six-pointed star (plate 11). This man is shown in a frontal position, with his head turned slightly to the right. He holds a small cylindrical item in his left hand while the right is lifted up to his chest. His robes are decorated with gold stripes in the highlights. The man and the star which almost merge because of their colour value, come forth from out of a circular mandorla of variegated blue. Thin gold lines radiate from the circle's centre.

Two men in three quarter profile stand on their respective mountain tops to the right and left of the man clad in white. The man on the left wears a greenish robe with dashes of ochre and blue, highlighted with white. He gives his attention to the central man by a gesture of his right hand. The somewhat younger man to the right is clothed in a reddish brown robe with light grey highlights. He holds a rectangular item with both hands. These men have blue tunics under their rich drapery.

Three blue lines stream from the circle and touch three men who lie curled up in the lower part of the picture. The man on the left turns his face upward and looks toward the man in white, while the central figure almost lies in a fetal position with his face turned downward. His chin is resting in his left hand as if he is in thought, while he stretches out his right hand in front as though protecting himself from the fall. Furthest to the right lies the third man — also he is curled into a ball, with one hand over his face, again, seeming to protect himself from the scene above. The colours of the clothing are, from left to right, orange, ocher brown with dashes of blue and plum-red with light blue highlights. All three have blue tunics with brown undertones.

Between the two main groups of three persons, we see two groups of four persons in smaller scale. The groups are framed in by cliffs forming a kind of enclosure in the mountain. They differentiate themselves from the surroundings by their dark clothing. A man with a halo walks in front of the others. He turns his head towards those who walk behind him. The group to the left is in the process of ascending the mountain, while the other group on the right is descending and leaving the scene. In the area between these four groups we find two dark caves in the mountain whose entrances are marked by a tree.

In the upper two corners of the picture there are blue-grey cloudlike forms, each with two small half-length figures. An angel painted with the same colours as the clouds, leads the figures who come down towards the three men on the mountain top. The two figures following the angels are kept in muted earth colours and seem as though they are reduced versions of the two men just beneath them.

Formal Analysis

Composition

The composition is built on symmetry and a rhythmic repetition of pictorial elements around a vertical central axis. The geometric forms which create the mid axis are a circle in the upper part of the picture and a pyramidal triangle in the lower. The compositional scheme is further developed by two smaller triangles that arise on each side behind the dominant one in the centre. These triangles correspond with the mountain tops described above. The figures are placed diametrically across from each other, be they ordered in groups or standing as separate individuals. These figurative components can be read as four horizontal parallel lines and three parallel vertical lines. In such a way we can visualize an invisible grid behind the composition. Since the picture has such a firm geometric underpinning, it gives the impression of stability and balance. It is the shining circle with the white-clad man in the top part of the picture together with the varied body positions that break this static pattern.

Depth and Perspective

A very noticeable trait of the picture is that it seems to be divided into three different areas comprised of three different episodes. Read in this way, the two small groups at the very top become a place far away, while the two slightly larger groups further down make a space closer to the viewer. The six figures making up the central episode would constitute the largest and closest space. Since all the episodes are presented on the same pictorial surface, it seems as though they happen simultaneously. The question is therefore if this also indicates three time periods; however, we cannot answer this before the episode is identified.

The pointed pyramidal shape of the mountains and the dominant circle in the upper part of the picture lead the eye upwards more than inwards. A sensation of depth is achieved in that the mountains overlap each other. Thus the two mountains that rise from behind the large central peak, at first glance seem further away, but this effect is contradicted since the three figures who stand on these peaks are the same size and act within the same space. In addition to this, the two apparently distant mountains have a warm, orange brown colour while the closer mountain is a cold green colour with some accents of turquoise.

There is not a proportionally correct relationship between landscape and figures. The figures dominate the landscape. An exception can be the two groups who are completely surrounded by mountains. But the largest figures do not look as though they have real contact with the ground — for that the mountains are too small and steep. The landscape functions almost as a stage for a carefully planned drama. Another feature which strengthens this impression is that the mountains are seen from above while the figures are viewed frontally.

The cave entrances indicate an opening into the mountain and are thus an expression of the mountain having volume. Yet further down the picture it is difficult to define the landscape. It seems as though the three men *hover over* the ground rather than lay on it. The green colour creates a type of neutral background for the figures. But since this lowest part of the picture is a natural extension of the central mountain, it can be read as a steep slope.

The figures have distinct contours and are given a sculptural form by strong colour contrasts in their clothing and skin. The exception here is the man in the mandorla. The drapery seems flat because the combination of gold on white has no contrasting effect. When this white and golden clothing appears against a background that is just as white and golden, it can seem from a distance difficult to differentiate between the person and the six-pointed star. More clearly seen are the head and hands. To conclude, it could reasonably be said that this spatial analysis reveals a dynamic relationship between the flat plane and depth, the picture presenting two rather than three dimensions.

Movement

In the discussion on composition it was said that the basic structure of the picture was static. Further it was noted that the bright man in the circle is an immediate focal point and thus functions as the energy field of the motif. These two aspects combine stability and dynamism. Movement arises first and foremost from dramatic body positions, in particular the three men at the bottom of the composition. They crouch, gesticulate, fall head-first to the ground or turn away from the blinding light. He who is the source of all these reactions stands calmly on his mountain top between two similarly calm figures, their bodies showing no outward drama.

Besides the above, we find movement in the four groups who, by being "on their way," create a diagonal movement within the picture. An interesting detail here is that behind the central figure in white, there is a circle within a circle which does not correspond directly with the one behind it. Because the two circles have different centres, the balance is disturbed. In this way tension arises within a form generally thought of as being static.

Colour

The colours have already been mentioned in the preceding text because the colours together with the organization of forms constitute the picture. It still remains to look at the colours as a whole. Some reflections on the egg tempera technique's unique qualities can also be included here.

The colouring can be roughly divided into two parts — the warm and the cold. The lower, warmer sphere is built up around the complementary colours of red and green. The upper colder sphere has white and blue as the main colours. A glowing gold background binds these two fields together. Each local colour is repeated one or more times. For instance, we can see different grades of blue in the two cloud formations, the circle, on the tunics and as highlights on some of the robes. It is a case of there always being variations within a colour category. For example, under the theme of red, we find orange, brown, plum red and magenta. The green colour can be tinted with blue or brown. This interrelated colouring can give the impression of the pictorial elements making an organic whole. The reason the colours can appear as they do is that the egg tempera technique demands several layers of paint in order for the colours to be opaque. The emulsion of egg yoke and water is partly transparent and therefore gives the colour a translucent look. This quality has been utilized by the painter letting one layer affect the other.

Light

The combination of colour and gilding in the upper part of the picture is an expression of the same tendency to let light slip through the material. The glowing white man who comes forth from a bright glowing star in a mandorla filled with light, functions both as focal point, energy field and light source. By reading the figures in the mentioned order, we can construct the following scheme: white with gold beams — on white with gold beams — on blue with gold beams — on a gilded background. We observe a desire to show the light in the most intense and complete form that this painting technique affords.

The light manifests itself in varied ways throughout the picture. The highlights on the mountains, clothing and skin are a result of light coming from different directions outside of the picture itself. This leads towards the confusion of space. The effect can be called *pseudolighting*. The *sent light* on the other hand comes from within, distributed through the gold and the transparent colours. In addition, an *internal sent light* comes from above in the form of three blue rays from the mandorla.

Identification

Even though there is a period of more than eight hundred years between the two previously discussed mosaics and this Russian icon, the presuppositions for identifying the motif are the same. It concerns being aware of actual iconographical conventions as well as relevant biblical and church-historical texts. The inscriptions can also be of help.

The icon tells the story of the transfiguration of Jesus on the mountain in a form corresponding to the current pictorial norm, such as it was expressed after the iconoclastic period. We see Jesus standing or almost hovering on the central peak with Elijah to the left and Moses to the right. Jesus holds a scroll in his left hand and blesses with his right. Between the halo and the shoulders there are the initials IC-XC — the first and last letters in the Greek spelling of Jesus Christ. This form was not changed with the introduction of Church-Slavonic inscriptions.

Moses holds the tablet of the law in his hands. In the lower part of the picture Peter is placed furthest to the left, John in the middle and James to the right. Except for the Cyrillic initials, which point out who is who, Peter is recognized by some conventional features. According to an early established tradition, Peter had short, grey, curly hair and beard. This marks Peter as the oldest of the twelve. In contrast to the two other disciples, he looks eagerly and animatedly towards the astonishing scene on the mountain top. As we know, the gospels describe how Peter in this situation took the initiative to suggest building tents for each of the three men. Mark adds that *"he did not know what to say, for they were exceedingly afraid"* (Mark 9:6). John and James both show more outward signs of the fear they all felt.

As mentioned under the topic of depth and perspective, there are two areas with two smaller figures in addition to the main motif. These groups complete the narrative aspect and give the action an introduction and conclusion. In the group on the left we see that *"Jesus took with him Peter and James and John, and led them up a high mountain"* (Mark 9:2). In the corresponding group to the right we can imagine Jesus admonishing his disciples: *"Tell no one the vision, until the Son of Man is raised from the dead"* (Matt. 17:9).

The two small groups at the top of the picture give us a glimpse into an existence that transcends the limited categories of time and space. Moses and Elijah are being brought from their heavenly dwellings by angels and led to a meeting with the glorified Son of God.

The Russian art historian Michael Albatov attributes this icon to Theophane the Greek, an icon and fresco painter who decorated churches, amongst other places at Novgorod and Moscow. This was during the late fourteenth and early fifteenth century. Other researchers attribute this work to the group of artisans working close to Theophane. The icon has a monumental format. It measures 184 × 134 cm and was painted in 1403 in connection with the restoration of the Cathedral of Transfiguration in Pereslavl-Zalleskij where it was meant to function as the titular icon of the cathedral.

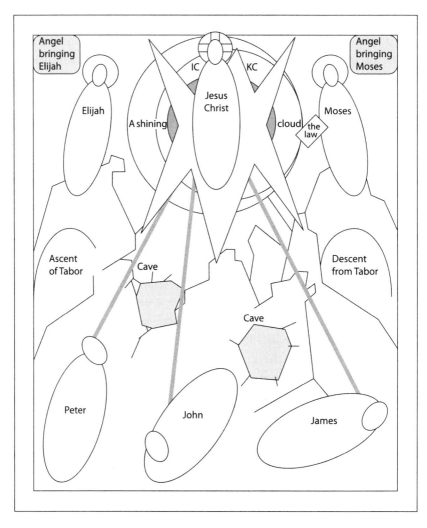

This model shows the identification of persons, groups, individual elements and inscriptions in the Russian Transfiguration icon.

Chapter II

THE VISION OF LIGHT

The Incarnation, with Reference
to the Ottonian Manuscript Illumination

The Incarnation as Basis for the Transfiguration

We shall see that the Incarnation is a theological prerequisite for the Transfiguration. The underlying connection between these events in the life of Jesus is implicitly apparent within the Transfiguration motif, but the events express themselves explicitly in the Old Testament. Here we find a juxtaposition of the birth of Jesus and his glorification in one painting — something very unusual in Byzantine art.[1] We have chosen this miniature instead of two conventional icons because we want to demonstrate how crucial the Incarnation is both as theological justification of the art of making icons and as the dogmatic basis for the Transfiguration. Even though

---

1. Towards the end of the tenth century and throughout the eleventh, the Ottonian court was influenced by the conventions of Byzantium. Distinguishing features of Ottonian art therefore also reveal aspects of their Byzantine precursors. The above statement that it is unusual to find two episodes from the life of Jesus in the same Byzantine painting, is said on the basis of the knowledge of how Byzantine conventions developed after iconoclasm. We know that much was lost during iconoclasm, but we do not know what these works looked like. Thus we cannot exclude the notion that the Ottonian miniature could resemble lost Byzantine works.

the Ottonian manuscript illumination in its form belongs to the Western church, its meaningful content is fully representative of Eastern theology.[2] We can furthermore perceive a certain formal pictorial language linking the Western Ottonian art and the Eastern Byzantine art of that time.[3]

At the top of the manuscript illumination, we see a representation of the birth of Jesus. The inscription written along the inside of the crib and continued in the area to the right where the three disciples are, describes the incarnation in brief: "The Word was made flesh and lived among us." This compressed representation of the birth of Jesus provides the basis for a similarly abbreviated depiction of the transfiguration of Jesus: *"we have beheld his glory, glory as of the only Son of the Father, full of grace and truth"* (John 1:14). This excerpt from the prologue of Saint John holds within itself the seed of the dogma of the two natures of Christ and underlines the close relationship between the Incarnation and the Transfiguration. In Bethlehem God clothes himself in man's nature, on Tabor he manifests his divine nature.

These two experiences in the life of Jesus are surrounded by extraordinary phenomena of light. In a homily "On the Holy Baptism" by Gregory of Nazianzus (ca. 330–381) the shining star over Bethlehem as well as the shining clouds at Tabor are connected to central theophanies in the Old and New Testament. Moses and Elijah, who both in their time experienced the divine presence in the form of light and fire, were also present in the vision of light that the disciples witnessed. Gregory begins by saying that "God is Light" and continues to discribe how light, which is, in fact, a main characteristic of God, time after time breaks into man's existence. This con-

---

2. Because of there being no iconoclasm in the West and no Renaissance in the East, the relationship between theology and iconography developed differently within the Western and Eastern churches. During the eighth and ninth century iconoclasm caused a theological defense of sacred art in the East which was never necessary in the West. During the Renaissance there occurred a thorough reorientation in the West which did not affect the East. Because of the strong tie between art and doctrine in the Eastern church, it was undesirable to adopt ideas which would separate these spheres from each other. Since this was not yet a problem for the tenth century, we can allow for a Western version of Jesus' birth and transfiguration to illustrate an Eastern view of these motifs.

3. The marriage between the Byzantine princess Theophano and the future emperor Otto II in 972 contributed towards the expansion of cultural contacts between the East and the West. See Eleanor Duckett, *Death and Life in the Tenth Century,* p. 92.

tinual prefiguration of "the true light" (John 1:9) came with the Incarnation. This light had the following effect:

> Moses' face was made glorious by it. And to mention more lights —
> it was light that appeared out of fire to Moses, when it burned the
> bush indeed, but did not consume it. . . . And it was light that was in
> the pillar of fire that led Israel and tamed the wilderness. It was light
> that carried Elias in the car of fire. . . . It was light that shone round
> the shepherds. . . . It was light that was the beauty of the star that
> went before to Bethlehem to guide the wise men's way. . . . Light was
> that godhead which was shown upon the mount to the disciples.[4]

Even though God hid his face from Moses on Sinai, the radiance was strong enough to make the face of Moses shine (Exod. 34:29-35). The same light appeared as a consuming fire on Carmel (I Kings 18:38). On the way from Carmel to Sinai via Bethlehem and up to Tabor we see that the face of God gradually was revealed and the light intensified. When Moses and Elijah converse face to face with God on Tabor, it is because God's personified radiance drew nigh through the incarnation. The shepherds in Bethlehem, the prophets and disciples on Tabor contemplate he who *"reflects the glory of God and bears the very stamp of his nature"* (Heb. 1:3).

The Incarnation as Basis for Deification

The motif of the Incarnation illustrates several basic theological thoughts which are deeply pondered in patristic literature. The sources are quite comprehensive so here it will be limited to just a few excerpts. We begin with a quote from the book "On the Incarnation" by Athanasius, bishop of Alexandria (328-373), which serves as a basis for the thoughts we will now present:

> God became man so that man could become god.

4. Gregory of Naziansus, "On the Holy Baptism," as quoted by Sirarpie der Nersessian in "The Illustrations of the Homilies of Gregory of Nazianzus, Paris gr. 510, A Study of the Connections between Text and Images," in Dumbarton Oak Papers, 1962, pp. 200-201.

This pregnant sentence holds a fundamental Christian insight about the relationship between God and man — here we find both a central theological and an anthropological point which inspires one to further reflection.

Athanasius emphasizes the Incarnation as a new beginning for ascension to and union with God. The bold formulation that man can *"become god"* is an echo of the words of Psalm 82:6 where it is written, *"You are gods."* The expression "god" (with small *g*) in this context refers to the process the Greek Church fathers called deification of man (theosis). It is not simply a question of a "restoration" of man's original nature or a return to man's state before the fall. The Incarnation contains a qualitative additional dimension in relation to the position Adam and Eve had in paradise. The consequences of the Incarnation are greater than merely being without sin.

When God became man in Christ, God took on man's nature such that man could partake of divine nature (II Pet. 1:4). God's descent to man (katabasis) is a prerequisite for man's ascent to God (anabasis). Man is called to be like God. In order for that to occur God had first to be like man. To be God-like can be realized by man's will being joined with God's grace (synergeia). Man can be understood as a psychophysical entity where body, soul and spirit are capable of deification. This holistic approach competed with various contemporary platonistic ideas which expressed a dualistic anthropology.

Through the Incarnation man is potentially lifted to a level which transcends the status he possessed in the garden of Eden. This radical rise in status applies also to the rest of creation — the whole cosmos is encompassed by God's union with matter. To place such importance on the Incarnation has consequences for our view of matter and man's body. To put it more directly: God also became a "body" when he became man. Disdain for the human body is therefore also disdain for the incarnate God.

A further development of this thought is the idea that the incarnate God after his ascension continues to live in the Church through the eucharist. The body and blood of Christ in the form of bread and wine is united with the body of the communicant and transforms him gradually into a greater likeness to God. The Latin word "sacrament" has its Greek equivalent in the word "mystery." By combining these words we have the following definition: "A holy action which unites man with God." Another definition which also says something about the eucharist's quality and effect can be formulated thus: "A visible sign that mediates God's invisible grace." The materiality of the sacrament actualizes and conveys the sanctifying effects of the incarnation. Partaking of the sacraments is thus one of several means of achieving "theosis."

Two other means which shall be mentioned in brief here are asceticism and prayer. The goal of ascetic exercises is a gradual liberation from the vices and development of the virtues. A large portion of ascetic literature is about how disciplining the body by asceticism and disciplining the mind by prayer prepare man for mystical union with God. This union can be experienced in glimpses already in this life. Such ecstatic moments are interpreted as eschatological signs which point towards the perfect life in the world to come. Nevertheless, a person who by a holy life fulfills his vocation of achieving likeness with God is a clearer sign of deification than a person who is subject to various supernatural experiences. The holy man or woman — the saint — exemplifies the goal of the Christian life and has thus an important function as model.

The relationship between the *incarnation* of God and the *theosis* of man can be explained as follows:

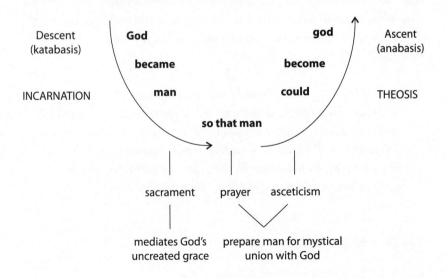

The Incarnation as Basis for the Art of Icon Painting

Since the divine descended into matter, it has received a sacred capacity which is clearly expressed within Orthodox art. By its spiritualized materiality, the icon refers simultaneously back to the incarnation as well as forward to the transfiguration and towards the transformed matter in the world to come. The icon can thus be understood both as a sacramental and an eschatological sign. While not a sacrament itself, it can be said to have a sacramental character because it combines matter and divine revelation. The apostle John emphasizes the aspect that God was perceptible in Christ when he writes:

> That which was from the beginning, which we have *heard,* which we have *seen* with our eyes, which we have *looked upon* and *touched* with our hands, concerning the word of life. (I John 1:1)

The Incarnation implies that God freely allowed himself to be made limited, subjected to time and space. The absolute transcendent and unattainable God became immanent and tangible. The uncreated and invisible God allows himself to be born into the created world and becomes visible. The Nicene Creed from A.D. 325 formulates the mystery of the Incarnation thus:

> We believe in one Lord, Jesus Christ, the only Son of God, eternally begotten of the Father, God from God, Light from Light, true God from true God, *begotten, not made,* of one Being with the Father. Through him all things were made. For us men and for our salvation he came down from heaven: by the power of the Holy Spirit he became incarnate of the Virgin Mary, and *was made man.*

The Incarnation and Iconoclasm

When the great apologists of icons, John of Damascus and Theodore the Studite, formulated the dogmatic legitimization of icons, they built their arguments on prevailing christology. The physical and the theological attack on icons during the Byzantine iconoclastic period made it necessary for a dogmatically founded theology of images. John of Damascus (ca. 675–ca. 749) wrote three apologetic treatises where point for point he answered the criticisms of the iconoclasts. In the last phase of iconoclasm these arguments were drawn out further by Theodore the Studite (759-826). The conflict, which lasted from 726 to 843, can be divided into two phases because the iconodule Empress Irene and her like-minded descendants ruled between 780 and 813. The definitions (resolutions) from the iconoclastic Council which the emperor Constantine V called together in Constantinople in 754 were declared null and void by the Seventh Ecumenical Council in Nicea in 787. The final triumph of the iconodules in 843 is still celebrated on the first Sunday of Lent under the name "The Triumph of Orthodoxy."

Emperor Leo III, who ruled at the beginning of the iconoclastic period in 726, used the Mosaic commandment against making images as the basis for his arguments. Figurative representations of Christ, the Mother of God and the saints were systematically destroyed, chopped, attacked, overpainted and burned, regardless of their being manuscript illuminations, frescoes, mosaics, icons or liturgical utensils. The Byzantine preiconoclastic mosaics in Ravenna and Sinai which are discussed in this study, escape the iconoclasts' destruction because they were outside the territory of the Byzantine empire. The danger lay not only in the threat of physical distruction, but also in the more profound consequences that iconoclastic thinking would result in dissolution of fundamental Christian teaching.

When the Iconodules were accused of idolatry, John of Damascus answers by claiming that the iconoclasts had, in fact, Manichean tendencies by their devaluation of matter. This is an indirect rejection of the Incarnation. He also directs sharp criticism at Emperor Leo III and his sympathizers who, without an ecclesiastical mandate, dictated to the Church, and he asks ironically: *"The Manicheans wrote the Gospel according to Thomas; will you now write the Gospel according to Leo?"*[5]

In his defense of icons, John of Damascus points out the unreasonableness of treating the law against images from the Old Covenant as if it

5. John of Damascus, *On the Divine Images*, II, 16, p. 63.

should be valid for the New Covenant, because, as he says, *"If you invoke the law in your despising of images, you might just as well insist on keeping the sabbath and practising circumcision."*[6] The law against making images given to the Jews has two easily understandable reasons; namely the absolute transcendence of God and the danger of idolatry. Moses warns the people against replacing God with an image of God, *"Then the Lord spoke to you out of the midst of the fire; you heard the sound of words, but saw no form; there was only a voice"* (Deut. 4:12). As long as God is unavailable through the senses, it is impossible to give God a recognizable form. If God lets his voice be heard, his nature is nevertheless unlimited and thus cannot be depicted either verbally or visually. All such attempts are a falsehood. Thus far the iconoclasts and the iconodules have common views.

How can the invisible be depicted? How does one picture the inconceivable? How can one draw what is limitless, immeasurable, infinite? How can a form be given to the formless? How can you describe a mystery?[7]

In his argumentation for the depiction of Christ, John of Damascus quotes the text from the New Testament which describes the transition from the Old to the New covenant, from the transcendent to the physically present God:

No one has ever seen God; the only Son, who is in the bosom of the Father, he has made him known. (John 1:18)

He who has seen me has seen the Father. (John 14:9)

He is the image (icon) of the invisible God. (Col. 1:15)

In many and various ways God spoke of old to our fathers by the prophets; but in these last days, he has spoken to us by a Son. (. . .) He reflects the glory of God and bears the very stamp of his nature. (Heb. 1:1-3)

6. Ibid., I, 16, p. 25.
7. Ibid., I, 8, p. 18.

On Sinai God permitted himself to be heard, but not seen. The Word had not yet become man. On Tabor God was both heard and seen. Since the perfect image of God, who *is* God, became man and allowed himself to be seen, heard and touched by man, it is legitimate to represent God in pictorial form. As we already mentioned, the rising status of matter is a natural consequence of the incarnation. Therefore it is also legitimate to honor matter as a divine medium of communication.

> In former times God, who is without form or body, could never be depicted. But now when God is seen in the flesh conversing with men, I make an image of the God who is seen in the flesh conversing with men, I make an image of the God whom I see. I do not worship matter; I worship the Creator of matter who became matter for my sake, who willed to take his abode in matter; who worked out my salvation through matter. Never will I cease honoring the matter which wrought my salvation. I honor it, but not as God.[8]

John of Damascus distinguishes between worship (latreia), which is only directed towards God, and veneration (proskynesis), which is directed towards what God communicates himself through. Here he bases his argument upon Basil the Great, who claims that *"the honour given to the image is transferred to its prototype."*[9] Athanasius of Alexandria expresses the idea in a similar way: *"He who bows to the icon bows to the King in it."*[10]

In connection with the iconoclastic council of 754, the debate turns away from the basic theological justification of icons towards more subtle, christological questions about the relationship between the icon of Christ and the two natures of Christ. What is it which is represented in an icon of Christ? Is it his divine or his human nature, or both? By asking this question the iconoclasts, with the emperor Constantine V at the head, present an apparently unsolvable dilemma. To represent the divine nature of Christ is impossible, to represent the human nature of Christ would fall into Nestorianism, to represent both would be a mixture of Christ's two natures

---

8. Ibid., I, 16, p. 23.
9. Ibid., I, 21, p. 29, quoted after Basil of Caesarea, "On the Holy Spirit."
10. Daniel J. Sahas, *Icon and Logos, Sources in Eighth-Century Iconoclasm*, p. 145.

and thus Monophysitism. All these alternatives would come into conflict with the christological definition from Calcedon (451) which states that the person of Christ was beheld in two natures *without confusion, unchanged, and without division."*

At the Seventh Ecumenical Council in Nicea in 787 this argument is turned against the iconoclasts. There is neither division nor confusion of the natures of Christ. The icon represents the person of Christ as he appeared as a human being. The iconodules defined the icon as a symbol (typos) which only fulfills its purpose when it transcends itself. A symbol is a symbol *for* something, it has a representational function. Therefore the icon is holy and deserves honor in reference to what it symbolizes. When Constantine V denounces the icon cult as heretical practice, it is because he does not consider the icon to be a symbol, but as being one with that which it represents. To the iconoclasts, the type and the prototype have the same essence. By making the icon autonomous, the symbolic function falls away and the icon comes to represent only itself. It becomes independent. When the icon is no longer a symbol, but replaces that which it is meant to represent, it is in danger of becoming an idol — a god.

Theodore the Studite dismisses this theory and says that it is idiocy to exchange the original with the copy, or Christ with an icon of Christ. The icon relates to Christ just as the shadow relates to the truth.[11] The icon partakes of the prototype through its similarity, not its identity. They bear the same name without having the same essence. The type is secondary and relative, the prototype is primary and absolute. Theodore the Studite also dismisses the iconoclastic emperor's claim that the eucharist is the only true and legitimate icon of Christ, because the eucharist *is* Christ, and not just a symbol.[12]

Word and Image

A defining feature of Orthodox theology which was emphasized by "The Triumph of Orthodoxy" is the consequent equality of word and image. The

---

11. Theodore the Studite, *On the Holy Icons,* I, 11, p. 31.
12. Ibid., I, 10, p. 30.

icon expresses visually what the gospel proclaims verbally. It is endowed with canonical authority in so far as it corresponds with the holy Scriptures and the Tradition of the Church. At the seventh Ecumenical Council in Nicea in 787 — also called Nicea II — the equality of sight and hearing is an integrated aspect in the defense of icons. Both senses can lead to knowledge of God and enlightenment of the mind:

> Thus, as when we receive the sound of reading with our ears, we transmit it to our mind, so by looking with our eyes at the painted icons, we are enlightened in our mind. Through two things following each other, that is, by reading and also by seeing the reproduction of the painting, we learn the same thing, that is, how to recall what has taken place.[13] That which the narrative declares in writing is the same as that which the icon does (in colours).[14]

> For that which speech presents through hearing by giving an account, painting does show, although silently, by the art of representation.[15] I saw an icon of the passion and I was not able to pass by the sight without tears, because the art was conveying the story vividly.[16]

These quotations emphasize the didactical function of icons. Both the stories written in the gospels and the painted representations teach and remind us of something. In order to give a basis for icons having an ecclesiastical authority, the council fathers claim that theology is a prerequisite of iconography. The visual representations reflect theophanies which already have occurred and thoughts already thought.

> The making of icons is not an invention of the painters, but an accepted institution and tradition of the catholic Church.[17] (. . .) The idea, therefore, and the tradition are theirs, not the painter's. Only

---

13. Daniel J. Sahas, *Icon and Logos,* p. 61.
14. Ibid., p. 69.
15. Ibid., p. 104 and 123, quoted after Basil of Caesarea.
16. Ibid., p. 143, quoted after Gregory of Nyssa.
17. The word "catholic" is here used in the general sense, meaning universal, conciliar.

the art is of the painter, whereas the disposition is certainly of the holy Fathers who erected (churches).[18]

Because the image has the same status as the word and the icon painter is subjected to the discipline of the Church, it becomes a reliable dogmatic source. Theology and iconography reflect and complete each other. There is created a trustworthiness of the iconographical material which is an adequate expression of the teaching of the Orthodox Church. A remarkable feature of the Byzantine traditional icons is its consistent conventional style. A tradition, however, is in principle a dynamic phenomenon allowing for development. Eventual changes of the way the motif is represented — and in this connection it is most relevant to mention the Transfiguration motif — can be understood as a result of a change in dogmatic emphasis. Consequently it is important to account for the theological context out of which Orthodox art arises.

"Urbild — Abbild"

Orthodox theology is permeated by the thought that the relationship between God and man is an "Urbild — Abbild" relationship (image — reflection). God is the original creator of images, the first artist who created "ex nihilo," from nothing. He creates man in his image, in his likeness (Gen. 1:27). God is the prototype, man is an imitation of the prototype. For as John of Damascus asks: *"How can what is created share the nature of him who is uncreated, except by imitation?"*[19]

Man came into being through the process of an image being created, and man's ability to create images is thus a reflection of the divine creativity. When a man makes an image of the incarnate God, it is a reflection of the process of creation of which he himself is a result. A transcription of the well-known words of the apostle John can illustrate this idea: "We create images because God created images first."[20] Man is formed in the image of

---

18. Daniel J. Sahas, *Icon and Logos*, p. 84.
19. John of Damascus, *On the Divine Images*, III, 20, p. 76.
20. I John 4:19: "We love him, because he loved us first."

God and *resembles* God, while the Son is the Father's *expressed* image and is God. As the expressed likeness of God, the Son is *the same as* the prototype, *"for he reveals the Father in his own person."*[21] Therefore it is written in the Nicene Creed that the Son is *"begotten, not created, of the same nature as the Father."*

The decisive division in life does not, as in Platonism, lie between spirit and matter, but between the created and the uncreated. Orthodox theology states a fundamental ontological division between the eternal, uncreated Creator, who exists in himself (in his own power), and all that is created which exists because of the Creator. By the Incarnation God became a creature without being created.

From Bethlehem to Tabor

The Ottonian manuscript illumination gives an abbreviated representation of God's gradual self-revelation. We see that the consequences of the Incarnation are all-embracing. The entire cosmos is incorporated into the mystery of salvation. Everything created, both the visible material world and the invisible spiritual world, is present in the image through the depiction of plants, animals, man, articles created by man such as clothing and the crib, a shining star and a host of angels. The spiritual sphere, represented by the angels over the fields of Bethlehem and the planets in the heavens, represented by the star shining over the stall, takes part in the drama of the Incarnation by making God visible for man, represented by the shepherds.

The cosmological consequences of the Incarnation are revealed in a glimpse for the disciples on Mount Tabor. They are blinded by a light which shone out from the transfigured Christ. The writers of the Gospel tell how the face and clothing of Christ shone with a supernatural energy. Within time we shall see that the light on Mount Tabor also has a transforming effect on its environment. The bodily transfiguration of Christ carries within it the hope of a future cosmological transfiguration. Among other things it is this aspect of the transfiguration of Jesus that the following chapter will discuss.

21. John of Damascus, *On the Divine Images*, III, 18, p. 75.

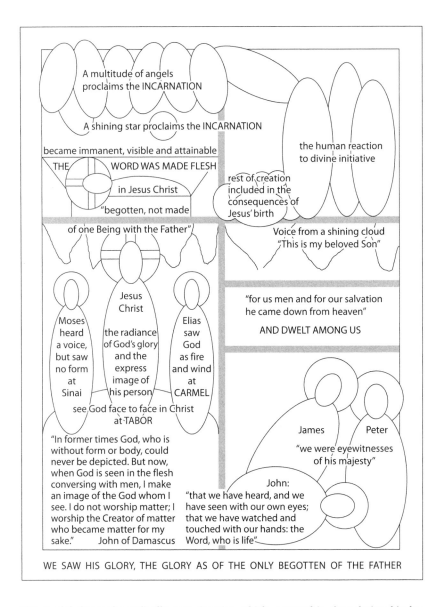

A multitude of angels proclaims the INCARNATION

A shining star proclaims the INCARNATION

became immanent, visible and attainable

THE WORD WAS MADE FLESH

in Jesus Christ

"begotten, not made

of one Being with the Father"

the human reaction to divine initiative

rest of creation included in the consequences of Jesus' birth

Voice from a shining cloud "This is my beloved Son"

Jesus Christ

the radiance of God's glory and the express image of his person

Moses heard a voice, but saw no form at Sinai

Elias saw God as fire and wind at CARMEL

see God face to face in Christ at TABOR

"for us men and for our salvation he came down from heaven"

AND DWELT AMONG US

James   Peter

"we were eyewitnesses of his majesty"

"In former times God, who is without form or body, could never be depicted. But now, when God is seen in the flesh conversing with men, I make an image of the God whom I see. I do not worship matter; I worship the Creator of matter who became matter for my sake."   John of Damascus

John: "that we have heard, and we have seen with our own eyes; that we have watched and touched with our hands: the Word, who is life"

WE SAW HIS GLORY, THE GLORY AS OF THE ONLY BEGOTTEN OF THE FATHER

This model shows the radically new situation which occurred in the relationship between the Creator and the creature through the Incarnation. On Tabor Moses and Elijah see face to face that which they earlier saw only indirectly. With the help of excerpts from the Nicene Creed, relevant quotes from the apostles Peter and John together with a quote from John of Damascus, the most central arguments for the legitimization of making images of the divine are recapitulated.

The Transfiguration, with Reference to the Mosaics in the Monastery of Saint Catherine in Sinai

Dogmatics and Mysticism

Within our chosen material the apsidal mosaic in the Monastery of Saint Catherine is the oldest example of a figurative representation of the Transfiguration. This monastery, which represents more that fourteen hundred years of almost continual liturgical life, is dedicated to both the Mother of God, Saint Catherine of Alexandria and the Transfiguration. By its geographical location, the Monastery of Saint Catherine is also connected with decisive events in the history of salvation where Moses was the main participant. Over the motif of the Transfiguration itself, we find references to the burning bush and the receiving of the law. Since Moses was present at both Mount Sinai and Mount Tabor, he contributes to the continuity of these theophanies and is a key person in the subsequent interpretations. It is difficult for us to know the intentions of those who designed and made the original decoration in the Monastery of Saint Catherine. Yet we can come to some understanding of it by studying excerpts from the theological traditional interpretation of the theophanies at Sinai and Tabor, as far as they had been developed up to that time.

The Transfiguration was understood quite early on as a dogmatic manifestation of the Trinity and of the two natures of Christ. These central dogmas received their most precise wording at the council of Nicea in 325 and Chalcedon in 451. The dogmas do not seem to be exhaustive theological definitions, but express, rather, limitations of a specific belief in a poetic style.

Vladimir Lossky regarded the sixth century as a time when the Church was more concerned with the consolidation of doctrine than mystical spirituality.[22] Without exception, dogmatic definitions which first were expressed in the conciliar texts were later grafted into the liturgy and expressed iconographically. But the scenes of theophanies from Sinai and Tabor communicate more than dogmatic postulates in visual form. Later we will see how the entire program of the decoration vibrates in the tension

22. Vladimir Lossky, *Vision of God,* p. 119.

between dogmatics and mysticism, between the confirmation of articles of faith and the striving towards high monastic ideals.

Positive and Negative Theology

In order to achieve a better understanding of the theological content, we will follow the same developmental process which the formula of Athanasius inspired in the paragraph on the Incarnation. We imagine a basic structure where movement proceeds from God down to mankind, after which it rises up again from man to God. Visually, this movement is creating a U-shape.

We begin thus with God. What can be deduced regarding the nature of God by reflecting upon the Transfiguration? Before we can answer this question, we must first tackle an epistemological problem: How can man know anything about God when the human and the divine represent two different spheres of existence? As a solution to this problem, the theological tradition of the Eastern church has two ways of knowledge or theological methods:

When we say that God is true, good and beautiful, these are positive, confirming attributes which say something about God by saying what he *is*. This way of knowledge is positive or kataphatic, and starts from man's ability to comprehend and acknowledge the natural world, translating it into knowledge of the divine. We draw conclusions from the immanent to the transcendent. Implicit in this method is that the positive qualities we attribute to God will always be incomplete because God always will be "greater than" and "more than" what we are able to say about him.

When we say that God is uncreated, unlimited, invisible, indescribable and unattainable, these are negative attributes which say something about God by saying what he *is not*. This way of knowledge is called negative or apophatic and has its origin in the fact that the transcendent nature of God lies outside what man can fathom. The paradoxical character of apophatic theology can be formulated as "knowledge about unknowledge" (agnosia). Such an agnostic standpoint does not imply that the way of knowledge about God is blocked, rather that man is dependent upon God to declare himself and to make himself known. God's appearance or theophany is a divine adaptation to human experience. How can the uncreated God communicate with the created man without adapting himself to the limitations of the receiver?

It is first and foremost the name Dionysius the Areopagite which comes to mind when presenting the apophatic theology. Dionysius the Areopagite is the pseudonym of a Christion philosopher who used Neoplatonistic terminology — most probably a Syrian monk — who was active towards the end of the fifth or the beginning of the sixth century.[23] The name itself is derived from the Dionysius who came to faith through Paul's speech to the Athenians at the Areopagos (Acts 17:22-34). This Pseudo-Dionysius was soon believed to be a spiritual authority both among Greek and Latin theologians and had a decisive influence on contemplative spirituality both in the Eastern and the Western church.

The Essence and the Energies of God

The Holy Scripture presents a paradox when it says that *"man shall not see me and live"* (Exod. 33:20) and *"Blessed are the pure in heart, for they shall see God"* (Matt. 5:8). By differentiating between the essence and the energies of God, apophatic theology maintains the tension between the unknown and the manifest God. God is absolutely transcendent, unfathomable and unattainable in his inner nature or essence (ousia), but reveals himself through his powers or energies (dynamis, energeia). The unknown God is described by negations, the manifest God by positive attributes.

A much used metaphor says that the essence is in relation to the energies of God as the sun is in relation to its rays. The rays of the sun mediate its qualities, which are light and heat, while the sun itself remains unattainable. God reveals himself in such a way that the receiver can withstand the energies just as the sun mediates itself in a tempered form through its rays. The energies do not represent a kind of watering down of the essence, but can be explained as a radiation where God is present. The essence is the cause, the energies are effects which are also integrated with the cause. God reveals his

---

23. Vladimir Lossky, *Vision of God*, p. 123. Here the theology of Dionysius the Areopagite is seen as a Christian correction of the philosophy of Plotinus.

presence by taking on a perceptible form — as in the bush which burned without being consumed. Yet God was not identical with this perceptible form.[24]

The burning bush which surprised Moses, the consuming fire at Sinai and Carmel, the chariot of fire which took Elijah up to heaven and the blinding light of Tabor are examples of the uncreated energies of God. In the mosaic we can see the gilded background, the mandorla and rays of light as iconographical expressions of these energies.

Divine Light and Divine Darkness

Gregory of Nyssa (ca. 335-395), who was most likely active about one hundred years before Dionysius the Areopagite began his authorship, divulges his familiarity with the use of negation as a method for approaching the ineffable mystery. In the books *The Life of Moses* by Gregory of Nyssa and *Mystical Theology* of Dionysius the Areopagite Moses is used as a model for one who seeks the contemplative life. Both interpret the ascent to the top of Mount Sinai as a spiritual journey where the mystic goes from light to darkness, from the known to the unknown, from kataphatic to apophatic theology. This allegorical interpretation causes one to presume that Dionysius could have read Gregory. The lack of biographical information precludes sure knowledge about this.

At the top left of the triumphal arch we see Moses and the burning bush at the base of Mount Sinai. This imbues the representation with an extra dimension by showing that the experience of Moses happened typo-

24. The understanding of God's energies as a radiance of God's essence reminds us of, but must not be confused with, the philosopher Plotinus's Neoplatonistic theory of emanation. Plotinus thinks of the universe as a hierachically ordered system where each phenomenon represents an emanation (radiation) from the divine principle "The One." For Dionysius existence is also strictly hierachical. He differentiates between three different levels of existence, with God highest, the angelic or heavenly hierarchy in the middle and the ecclesiastical hierarchy lowest. Each level partakes of the divine "according to its portion." Within Plotinus' system the divine presence will diminish and the degree of materiality increase in proportion to the distance from the source of radiation. This view of matter stands in contrast to the Judeo-Christian teaching of creation as "very good" (Gen. 1:31), the dogma of the Incarnation and the self-giving of God through the sacraments.

graphically just outside of the monastery church. The chapel of the burning bush stands just a little to the left of the apse. It is a matter of the theophany "in situ" — at the site. Gregory writes:

> And if the flame by which the soul of the prophet was illuminated was kindled from a thorny bush, even this fact will not be useless for our inquiry. For if truth is God and truth is light — the Gospel testifies by these sublime and divine names to the God who made himself visible to us in the flesh — such guidance of virtue leads us to know that light which has reached down even to human nature. Lest one think that the radiance did not come from a material substance, this light did not shine from some luminary among the stars but came from an earthly bush and surpassed the heavenly luminaries in brilliance.[25]

Gregory is one of the first Church fathers who interprets the burning bush as a prefiguration of the Incarnation. Mary, the Mother of God, is *"an earthly bush"* who after having been ignited by the divine fire, *"radiated brighter than the heavenly lights."* The heavens could not contain he who allowed himself to be enclosed in the womb of Mary. The bush burned without being consumed. Mary bore and gave birth to God without being destroyed by the divine presence.

The meeting with the divine light in the burning bush represents the beginning of the ascent towards God. Again we see how the fact that God descended — *"all the way down to human nature"* — provides the basis for man's ascent towards God. However, before the actual ascent can begin, man needs to be cleansed from the consequences of the fall. Both Gregory and Dionysius divide the mystical experience into three classical stages — namely *cleansing* (catharsis), *enlightenment* (photismos) and *union* (henosis). Gregory continues:

> That light teaches us what we must do to stand within the rays of the true light: Sandaled feet cannot ascend that height where the light of truth is seen, but the dead and earthly covering of skins, which was

25. Gregory of Nyssa, *The Life of Moses*, 20, p. 59.

placed around our nature at the beginning when we were found naked because of disobedience to the divine will, must be removed from the feet of the soul.[26]

After cleansing follows enlightenment. There is a combination of these two phases presented in the mosaics where Moses stands by the burning bush and loosens his sandals. At the same time he turns his face towards the voice from above. He reacts to the revelation by freeing himself from that which can hinder him from getting closer to the mystery.

> It seems to me that at the time the great Moses was instructed in the theophany he came to know that none of those things which are apprehended by sense perception and contemplated by the understanding really subsists, but that the transcendent essence and cause of the universe, on which everything depends, alone subsists.[27]

God presents himself for Moses with the name "I Am" (Exod. 3:14). Only God *is* in the most basic meaning of the word. Moses is made to understand that the uncreated Creator, who having given all creation existence, exists in a different mode than the created. The uncreated fire made the bush burn without being consumed. When the uncreated fire illuminates a person, he is transformed into a greater likeness of God without thereby losing his identity.

At the upper right of the triumphal arch we see that Moses receives the commandments on the top of Mount Sinai. In contrast to the situation at the burning bush, Moses turns his face away from the hand which appears in the half circle. Moses is a passive receiver, his gaze is inward and his face has an absent expression. He both sees and does not see. The first time Moses meets God, it is in a burning flame,[28] the second time in a heavy cloud[29] and the third time in a thick darkness.[30] The closer Moses approaches God, the greater the darkness.

---

26. Ibid., 22, pp. 59-60.
27. Ibid., 24, p. 60.
28. Exod. 3:2: "he looked, and lo, the bush was burning, yet it was not consumed."
29. Exod. 19:16: "a thick cloud upon the mountain"
30. Exod. 20:21: "Moses drew near to the thick darkness where God was."

As the mystic seeks union with *"the transcendent essence and the universe's origin upon which everything is dependent,"* apophatic theology becomes his language. Dionysius the Areopagite uses the phrase "the divine darkness" or "the darkness of unknowing" when he discusses that which can not be spoken of. Man has neither the knowledge nor the language which can describe the essence of God. To seek union with the transcendent God entails all positive knowledge about the divine. Dionysius reminds us about this prerequisite when he says:

> leave behind the senses and the operations of the intellect, and all things sensible and intellectual (. . .) that thou mayest arise by unknowing (agnosia) towards the union (henosis), as far as attainable, with him who transcends all being and all knowledge. For by the unceasing and absolute renunciation of thyself and of all things thou mayest be borne on high, through pure and entire self-abnegation, into the superessential radiance of the divine darkness.[31]

> Nevertheless, he did not attain to the presence of God himself; he saw not him (for he cannot be looked upon) but the place where he dwells. And this I take to signify that the divinest and highest things seen by the eyes and contemplated by the mind are but the symbolical expressions of those that are immediately beneath him who is above all. Through these, his incomprehensible presence is manifested upon those heights of his holy places (. . .) and plunges the mystic into the darkness of unknowing, whence all perfection of understanding is excluded, and he is enwrapped in that which is altogether intangible and noumenal, being wholly absorbed in him who is beyond all, (. . .) and through the inactivity of all his reasoning powers is united by his highest faculty to him who is wholly unknowable.[32]

At the base of the mountain, before the ascent begins, Moses is surrounded by a divine light. He is active and striving. The theological method is

---

31. Dionysius the Areopagite, *Mystical Theology,* I, p. 9.
32. Ibid., p. 11.

kataphatic. At the top of the mountain, when the purpose of the ascent is achieved, Moses is enveloped in a divine darkness. He is passive and receptive. The theological method is apophatic.

Because the ascent is directed towards the infinite God, the ascent itself is also in principle unlimited. The spiritual growth or deification which begins in this life and continues in the next, is thus unending. Gregory explains:

> Such an experience seems to me to belong to the soul which loves what is beautiful. Hope always draws the soul from the beauty which is seen to what is beyond, always kindles the desire for the hidden through what is constantly perceived. Therefore, the ardent lover of beauty, although receiving what is always visible as an image of what he desires, yet longs to be filled with the very stamp of the arche - type.[33]

Here we see how the mystic moves from the visible to the invisible, from the reflection of beauty to that which is intrinsically beautiful. Deification (theosis) is a dynamic process, not a static state of being. The goal is not to come to a final destination, but to continually surpass new limits. Gregory summarizes the mystical experience thus:

> This truly is the vision of God: never to be satisfied in the desire to see him. But one must always, by looking at what he can see, rekindle his desire to see more. Thus, no limit would interrupt growth in the ascent to God, since no limit to the Good can be found nor is the increasing desire for the Good brought to an end because it is satis - fied.[34]

33. Gregory of Nyssa, *The Life of Moses,* 231, p. 114.
34. Ibid., 239, p. 116.

Moses as Model for the Monk

Towards the end of the text of *The Life of Moses* Gregory reveals the didactic reason for his writing:

> These things concerning the perfection of the virtuous life (. . .) we have briefly written for you, tracing in outline like a pattern of beauty the life of the great Moses so that each one of us might copy the image of the beauty which has been shown to us by imitating his way of life. (. . .) we consider becoming God's friend the only thing worthy of honor and desire. This, as I have said, is the perfection of life.[35]

The two representations of Moses remind the monks at the Monastery of Saint Catherine that they are literally walking on holy ground historically and geographically. In addition to illustrating that which *has happened,* the mosaics have a didactic function by emphasizing that which *can happen* using Moses as a model for the monastic life. Like Moses the monks have withdrawn into the loneliness of the desert in order to seek God and strive after *"the perfection of life."* Moses serves as a model both for the cenobitic monk who lives a sacramental and liturgical life within the community of the monastery and for the contemplative hermit who comes to church once a week in order to celebrate the eucharist. Moses himself alternated between life in a community and the life of a hermit.

The Heavenly and the Earthly Liturgy

As we have mentioned earlier, the lamb at the apex of the triumphal arch is both the compositional and thematic centre between the scenes of Moses and the Transfiguration. This is Christ as the sacrificial lamb, prefigured in the Mosaic tradition of sacrifice, announced by John the Baptist and worshipped by angels in heaven. Beneath the angels we find two medallions with portraits earlier identified as John the Baptist to the left and Mary to

---

35. Ibid., 319 and 320, pp. 136-137.

the right. When we look at these medallions together, we see the oldest deesis-group in Byzantine iconography and the only version with the lamb as the symbol of Christ. In later, more developed versions of the deesis-group the archangels Michael and Gabriel are found amongst the apostles and the spiritual fathers. The two angels who turn towards the lamb with the symbols of victory in their hands are not named, but can be associated these archangels. The apostles and prophets who flank the motif of the transfiguration can also be seen in relation to the picture field above. We can in this way surmise that here we have a glimpse of the heavenly liturgy which according to the visions in the Revelation of Saint John is centred around the worship of the lamb. This mid-pictorial field together with those representing the Old and New covenants constitute a "Urbild — Abbild" relationship where the heavenly liturgy is understood as an archetype of the earthly liturgy. The chuch on earth is an icon of the church in heaven.

The earthly liturgy centres around the lamb in the celebration of the eucharist. The eucharistic sacrifice actualizes the saving effects of Christ's sacrificial death. The archetypical sacrificial lamb reflects itself in the bread and wine which is offered on the altar directly beneath the centre of the triumphal arch. *The sacramental function* of the mosaic can be read in this way.

Diadochos of Photiki (ca. 400–ca. 486) encourages the monk to participate in the heavenly liturgy as a goal for the spiritual life while still here on earth. He writes that "The love of God's goodness embraces our intellect with the light of a transforming fire, and so makes it *a partner of the angels in their liturgy.*"[36]

Promise and Fulfillment

While we concern ourselves with the lamb as a symbol for Christ, we can mention that the Orthodox Church at the Council of Trullo in 692 prohibited the representation of Christ as a lamb. The Council fathers claimed that the dogma of Christ having come in human form was too diffuse by

---

36. Diadochos of Photiki, *Spiritual Knowledge and Discrimination*, 67, *The Philokalia*, Vol. I, p. 275.

such an indirect representation. This is why we do not find the lamb used as a symbol for Christ in Byzantine iconography after this prescriptive statement was formulated. In canon 82 of the Council text it says:[37]

> On some venerable images is depicted a lamb at whom the Forerunner points with his finger: this has been accepted as a symbol of Grace, showing us in advance, through the Law, the true Lamb, Christ our Lord.[38] While embracing the ancient *symbols and shadows* inasmuch as they are *signs and anticipatory tracings* handed down to the Church, we give preference to the Grace and the Truth which we have received as the fulfilment of the Law.[39] Consequently, in order that the perfect should be set down before everybody's eyes even in painting, we decree that (the figure of) the Lamb, Christ our God, who removes the sins of the world, should henceforward be set up in human form on images also, in the place of the ancient lamb,[40] inasmuch as we comprehend thereby the sublimity of the humiliation of God's Word, and are guided to the recollection of his life in the flesh, his passion and his salutary death, and the redemption which has thence accrued to the world.

By using words like "symbol," "shadow," "sign" and "anticipatory tracing" about the lamb which John the Baptist points towards, the Council text emphasizes that the transition from the *promise* of the first covenant to the *fulfillment* in the second covenant is a watershed in the history of salvation which has not only theological, but also iconographical consequences. The dogma of the incarnation as the argument for a figurative representation of Christ would be further developed and specified at the seventh ecumenical council at Nicea about one hundred years later.

---

37. Cyril Mango, *The Art of the Byzantine Empire, 312-1453, Sources and Documents,* pp. 139-140.

38. The Old Covenant, of which John the Baptist was the last representative.

39. John 1:17: "For the law was given through Moses; grace and truth came through Jesus Christ."

40. John 1:29: "Behold, the Lamb of God, who takes away the sin of the world."

The Old and the New Covenant

If we look at the entire decorative program simultaneously, we can deduce a *soteriological axis* from the top to the bottom. This axis reveals a divine plan of salvation where the episodes of the Old Testament are prefigurations for those in the New Testament. Within such a frame of reference scenes of Moses can be interpreted as typological prefigurations for the Incarnation and the Transfiguration. The burning bush is an analogy for the birth of Jesus in Bethlehem, as is the appearance on Mount Sinai analogous for the transfiguration of Jesus on Mount Tabor.

The portrait medallions with John the Baptist and Mary are placed in relation to the transfiguration motif itself with John the Baptist near Elijah and Mary near Moses. John the Baptist, who is named "the New Elijah," resembles his spiritual forefather by a zealous desire for God and by rebuking the authorities. Both practiced an extreme form of asceticism which has inspired many subsequent ascetics. Mary is associated with Moses because the burning bush typifies her as the one who gives birth to God (Theotokos). Mary with the honorable title "Mother of God," also called "the New Eve," gave birth to the Son of God, also called "the New Adam." These typological relationships reaffirm the continuity between the Old and the New Covenant. The historical continuity comes also to the fore by placing the transfiguration of Jesus in the midst of apostles and prophets. The apostles are witness to that which the prophets looked forward to — namely the appearance of God in human form.

Centrally placed between the prophets we find king David. Kurt Weitzmann points out an interesting detail when he claims that the beardless King David here borrows the facial characteristics of Emperor Justinian from the mosaic in San Vitale in Ravenna. According to the iconographical conventions, King David should have a beard in order to differentiate him from King Solomon with whom he is often pictured. Emperor Justinian has so to speak smuggled a portrait of himself into the row of prophets.[41] The imperial entrepreneur hides himself behind the mask of King David — the greatest king of Israel and the forefather of Jesus. Justinian is aware that he

---

41. George Forsyth and Kurt Weitzmann, *The Monastery of Saint Catherine at Mount Sinai, The Church and Fortress of Justinian*, p. 15.

is emperor "by the grace of God." He has his mandate from God and the ideal he should live up to is King David. Moreover, this indirect way of putting himself within the ranks of spiritual heroes witnesses to the fact of a powerful emperor who knew how to strengthen his own position within both the religious and political sphere.

As Moses in his time threatened Pharaoh with the judgement of God, so also Elijah rebuked Jezebel and John the Baptist, King Herod. The portait of King David alias Emperor Justinian ties Byzantium to the tradition in ancient Israel where the prophet could rebuke the king. This rule should ensure balance between the sacred represented by the prophet and the profane represented by the king. The imperial portrait in the Sinai mosaic can be interpreted as a fitting example of the relationship between the political and religious power in Byzantium while simultaneously confirming the Church as the new arena for the saving works of God.

The Transfiguration as Dogmatic Statement

The vertical axis along the centre of the composition can be seen as the *christological axis*. At the apex of the triumphal arch we find the medallions containing the lamb of God and the cross of Christ. In the apse we see the glorified Son of God inscribed in a blue mandorla while at the bottom is the portrait medallion with David, the human forefather of Jesus. This introduction reveals to us the two natures of Christ.

The human nature is seen most clearly in the three medallions at each end of the axis. The lamb and the cross illustrate the conversation between Moses, Elijah and Jesus when they spoke "of his passing which he was to accomplish in Jerusalem" (Luke 9:31). Only an incarnate God can suffer and die. The portrait of David reminds us of the lineage of Jesus' family, who *"descended from David according to the flesh"* (Rom. 1:3). The divine nature is revealed for the disciples at Tabor as they are witness to the transfiguration and hear the voice which sounds from the cloud of light: *"This is my beloved Son, with whom I am well pleased; listen to him"* (Matt. 17:5).

The dogma of the two natures of Christ demonstrates how the descent (katabasis) is a prerequisite for the ascent (anabasis), how the Incarnation is a prerequisite for the Transfiguration. This thought coinsides with the Ushaped structure which was explained earlier. The apostle Paul sums up the christological mystery thus:

> Christ Jesus, who, though he was in the form of God, did not count equality with God a thing to be grasped, but emptied himself, taking the form of a servant, being born in the likeness of men. And being found in human form he humbled himself and became obedient unto death, even death on a cross. Therefore God has highly exalted him and bestowed on him the name which is above every name. (Phil. 2:6-9)

The Trinity is another central dogma implicitly connected with the Transfiguration. At the baptism of Jesus the Father presents the Son in a similar manner as at his transfiguration; the difference being that at the baptism of Jesus *"the Holy Spirit decended upon him in bodily form, as a dove"* (Luke 3:22). The third person in the Godhead is also present at Tabor, but shows himself in another form, namely that of *"a bright cloud."* The disciples hear the Father, see the Son and are enveloped by the Holy Spirit.

In a commentary on the Transfiguration Origen of Alexandria (ca. 185–ca. 254) interprets the cloud of light both as a prefiguration of the resurrection and as an unveiling of the Trinity.[42] The nearest iconographical reference to the Trinity is the three circles which make up the background of the medallion incribed within the cross.

The Transfiguration as Eschatological Sign

When we turn our attention from the representation of Moses on the triumphal arch to the scene of the Transfiguration in the apse, we again are

---

42. Origen, *Commentary on the Gospel of Matthew*, The Ante-Nicene Fathers, Volume X, 42, p. 473. "That it (the bright cloud) might be to them a pattern of the resurrection to come, (...) But what might the bright cloud, which overshadows the just, be? 1. Is it, perhaps, the fatherly power, from which comes the voice of the Father bearing testimony to the Son as beloved and well-pleasing, (...) 2. And perhaps, too, the Holy Spirit is the bright cloud which overshadows the just, and prophesies of the things of God, who works in it, (...) 3. but I would venture also to say that our Saviour is a bright cloud."

met by Moses. The same Moses who, on Sinai, sought to see the transcendent God face to face, is shown on Tabor conversing face to face with he who *"reflects the glory of God and bears the very stamp of his nature"* (Heb. 1:3). Moses has reached his goal. Together with Elijah he refers to the Old Covenant, confirms the New Covenant and points towards the contemplation of God in the age to come.

John Chrysostom[43] (344-407) dwells on the idea of a gradual revelation of the mystery when he interprets the theophany at Sinai as a prefiguration of the theophany at Tabor which again is a prefiguration of the second coming of Christ. In a homily on the Transfiguration this eschatological aspect is described in the following way:

> But if we will, we shall also behold Christ, not as they then on the mount, but in far greater brightness. For not thus shall he come hereafter. For whereas then, to spare his disciples, he disclosed only so much of his brightness as they were able to bear; hereafter he shall come in the glory of the Father, not with Moses and Elias only, but with the infinite hosts of the angels, with the archangels, with the cherubim, with those infinite tribes, not having a cloud over his head, but even heaven itself being folded up.[44]

What the disciples glimpsed at Tabor will be thoroughly unfolded when the uncreated light breaks through into the created world. The uncreated light affects everything it touches and transforms the saints into the likeness of that which they see. The apostle John, who was eyewitness to the transfiguration, emphasizes this future perspective when he writes: "We know that, when he shall appear, we shall be like him; for we shall see him as he is" (I John 3:2). Dionysius the Areopagite's vision of the glory of the world to come can be understood as a paraphrase in the following text:

---

43. The name Chrysostom means "gold mouth" and reflects his remarkable exegetical and rhetorical capabilities. In addition to his penetrating biblical commentaries and pedagogically designed homilies, he is also renowned for having written a liturgy which is still in use in the Orthodox Church.

44. John Chrysostom, "Homily 56," The Nicene and Post-Nicene Fathers, Volume X, p. 349.

when we have arisen incorruptible, immortal, and have attained the blessed Christ-like state, we shall be, as the Scripture says, "for ever with the Lord," filled, through the all-pure and holy contemplation, with the visible manifestation of God himself, shining through us with most radiant splendour, as it shone about the disciples in the Transfiguration.[45]

Here we arrive at the fulfillment of the Christian promise of glory. The *eschatological vision* in the coming life is a completion of the *mystical vision* in this life.

Liturgical Time and Liturgical Space

The historical persons and episodes represented in the Sinai mosaic existed in another time and another space, while the angels and saints in heaven exist outside of time and space. The historical event on Tabor involved a manipulation of time and space in that Moses and Elijah *"appeared in glory"* (Luke 9:31). They were transported from the past (each from his own time), or in other words from a state which transcends time and space, and presented to the disciples in the present.

Through the liturgical practice, i.e. through the recitation of the holy texts — the office — and celebration of the holy rituals — the sacraments — the distance in time and space is nullified such that the meaning of the texts and rituals becomes immediate. Those who participate in the liturgy can be said to be included in a dimension of experience transforming "there and then" to "here and now." The liturgical practice is placed in a *liturgical space* and brings with it its own category of time which we can call *liturgical time*.

The impression of timelessness in the scene of the Transfiguration is expressed with the help of various iconographical effects such as the gilded background, the frozen movements and the lack of perspective. The evangelists tell that Jesus took the disciples with him *"up to a high mountain"* (Matt. 17:1). In the mosaic the landscape is reduced to three thin strips of

---

45. Dionysius the Areopagite, *Divine Names,* I, p. 12.

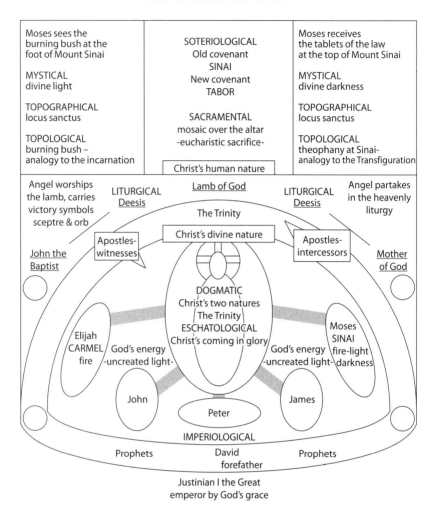

Moses sees the burning bush at the foot of Mount Sinai	SOTERIOLOGICAL	Moses receives the tablets of the law at the top of Mount Sinai

Moses sees the burning bush at the foot of Mount Sinai

MYSTICAL
divine light

TOPOGRAPHICAL
locus sanctus

TOPOLOGICAL
burning bush –
analogy to the incarnation

SOTERIOLOGICAL
Old covenant
SINAI
New covenant
TABOR

SACRAMENTAL
mosaic over the altar
-eucharistic sacrifice-

Christ's human nature

Moses receives
the tablets of the law
at the top of Mount Sinai

MYSTICAL
divine darkness

TOPOGRAPHICAL
locus sanctus

TOPOLOGICAL
theophany at Sinai-
analogy to the Transfiguration

Angel worships
the lamb, carries
victory symbols
sceptre & orb

LITURGICAL
Deesis

Lamb of God

The Trinity

LITURGICAL
Deesis

Angel partakes
in the heavenly
liturgy

John the
Baptist

Apostles-
witnesses

Christ's divine nature

Apostles-
intercessors

Mother
of God

DOGMATIC
Christ's two natures
The Trinity
ESCHATOLOGICAL
Christ's coming in glory

Elijah
CARMEL
fire

God's energy
-uncreated light-

Moses
SINAI
fire-light
darkness

God's energy
-uncreated light-

John

Peter

James

IMPERIOLOGICAL

Prophets

David
forefather

Prophets

Justinian I the Great
emperor by God's grace

colour. This abstraction has the effect of lifting the vision at Tabor out of a particular time and space and gives the scene validity for all times and all places. The mystery of the Transfiguration is actualized above and beyond the limited historical frame of reference.

Each time the feast of the Transfiguration is celebrated, the event takes place in the liturgical room of the monks. As mentioned in connection with the formal analysis, the concave apse gives the figures on Tabor a physical area in which to act. Through the intermingling of liturgy and iconography, time and space can be experienced as being suspended. The space is "here" and the time is "now." The Transfiguration at Tabor becomes the Transfiguration in the monastic church at Sinai. The Church repeats liturgically what Christ did historically.

Such a liturgical actualization has a sacramental character. The celebration of the eucharist is a contemporization of a holy act from the past. In

that the Church celebrates the eucharist "in remembrance of" (Luke 22:19) the last supper, a divine presence is mediated. When the monks recite the texts "in remembrance of" the Transfiguration, they are reminded of that which happened on Tabor once in the past, while the divine presence in the texts is tied to the present because God *is*.

On the basis of the interpretation we have given of the Sinai mosaic, we can establish the model on page 72.

The Transfiguration, with Reference to the Mosaic in Sant Apollinare in Classe in Ravenna

From Sinai to Ravenna

The transition from the mosaic in the Monastery of Saint Catherine in Sinai to the mosaic in Sant Apollinare in Ravenna is remarkable because the same motif is treated in such a very different way. We go from a thoroughly figurative to a completely symbolic representation of the Transfiguration. The architectural framework into which the mosaic is placed is however quite similar. Both buildings were erected and decorated during the reign of Emperor Justinian, and the theological basis for an interpretation of the Transfiguration which was explained in connection with the Sinai mosaics is also relevant for the Ravenna mosaics. However, a further comparison must wait until we have looked closer at that which is unique to the mosaic in Sant Apollinare in Classe.

The explanation of the complicated political situation of the time is not possible within the framework of this study. Suffice it therefore for us to comment on the prominent position of Bishop Apollinaris, a prevailing authority of the church's hierarchy, and Archbishop Maximian's politico-religious ambitions. At that time Ravenna was marked by rivalry between the pope's Rome and the emperor's Constantinople. Maximian was archbishop in Ravenna from 546 to 556 and functioned as Emperor Justinian's long arm within the western part of the Byzantine Empire. In order to ensure Ravenna's ecclesiastical and political pre-eminence, it was important to tie the city to the apostolic tradition. This poignant link was found in a legendary source who claimed that Apollinaris was ordained as bishop by the apostle Peter.[46] If the story is doubtful, the principle of authority is clear enough. As Ignatius of Antioch (ca. 112) says, *"Where the bishop is, there is the church."*[47] With reference to the mosaic in Sant Apollinare in Classe we can rewrite the quotation thus: *"Where the shepherd is, there are the sheep."*

---

46. This information is gathered from Otto G. von Simson, *Sacred Fortress, Byzantine Art and Statecraft in Ravenna*, pp. 40-62.

47. Ignatius of Antioch, "Epistle to the Smyrnaeans," quoted from *Documents of the Christian Church*, selected and edited by Henry Bettenson, pp. 63-64.

Since the entire decorative scheme dates from various periods, we shall primarily concentrate on the original mosaics, in other words, the main motif, the four bishops in the apse, the palm trees and the archangels on the triumphal arch. The remaining pictorial areas are additions which have less relevance.

The Glory of the Cross

The uniqueness of the monumental scene in the apse is this, that we stand in front of a combination of several motifs which are interrelated and which refer to different times, places and situations. Earlier we have identified the mosaic as the transfiguration of Jesus and the holy Apollinaris in glory, but the medallion of the cross also indicates the suffering, death, resurrection and second coming of Jesus.

The centrally placed medallion of the cross is an integral element in all motifs mentioned in this study and is therefore decisive in the way these motifs are interpreted. Where the arms of the cross intersect each other we see the face of Christ. This face *"shone like the sun"* at Tabor (Matt. 17:2). The cross is referred to indirectly on Tabor in the conversation between Christ and the two prophets. Luke tells us that they *"spoke of his departure, which he was to accomplish at Jerusalem"* (Luke 9:31). John Chrysostom reasons that one of the many purposes for the Transfiguration is *"To show the glory of the cross, and to console Peter and the others in their dread of the passion, and to raise up their minds."*[48] Pope Leo the Great (ca. 390–461) touches on the same idea when he reflects upon why the disciples were allowed to take part in such an overwhelming experience:

> And in this Transfiguration the foremost object was to remove the offence of the cross from the disciples' hearts, and to prevent their faith from being disturbed by *the humiliation* of his voluntary passion by revealing to them *the excellence* of his hidden dignity.[49]

48. John Chrysostom, "Homilies on the Gospel of Saint Matthew," Homily 56, The Nicene and Post-Nicene Fathers, Volume X, p. 346.

49. Leo the Great, "Homily 51," The Nicene and Post-Nicene Fathers, Volume XII, p. 163.

In a homily over the passion of Christ Leo the Great calls the cross *"a sceptre of power," "a trophy of triumph"* and *"an adorable sign of salvation."* He speaks of *"the most holy degradation"* of Christ and that *"the glory of the cross illuminates heaven and earth."*[50] The paradoxical expression *"the glory of the cross"* which both these exegetes use is a fitting description of how the cross appears on the mosaic in Sant Apollinare in Classe. To depict the transfigured Christ as a face on a bejeweled cross indicates that the cross has been transformed — a transfiguration — from an instrument of torture to a symbol of victory. In addition to being a prefiguration of the resurrection and the second coming of Jesus, the transfiguration also is a forewarning of his death. The medallion of the cross is ambiguous and is a symbol with many layers of meaning which demonstrate the inner cohesiveness of these events. Again we meet the christological theme which entails descent (katabasis) as a precondition for ascent (anabasis).

The historian Eusebius describes how the emperor Constantine the Great while on a military campaign saw a cross in the heavens and heard a voice which said: *"By this sign you shall conquer."*[51] Not long after, the emperor's mother Helena found the holy cross in Jerusalem. When the church later introduced a separate feast day for the exultation of the cross, it was as a result of a preestablished cult which had already arisen around this relic. The medallion of the cross has thus an explicit liturgical actuality each time the feast of the exultation of the cross is celebrated.

Martyrdom and Mystery

We notice that there are gradual transitions from one motif to the next. The three sheep that look up at the cross symbolize the disciples who gaze at the transfigured Christ. Since they take up part of the same pictorial space as the bishop Apollinaris, we can assume that they are present both at Tabor and in paradise. In the same way the bishop Apollinaris is present both in paradise and at Tabor because he shares the landscape with the disciples.

---

50. Ibid., "Homily 59," p. 172.
51. Eusebius, *The Life of Constantine,* The Nicene and Post-Nicene Fathers, Volume I, p. 490.

Plate 1. The Transfiguration, apse mosaic at the Monastery of Saint Catherine in Sinai (565)

Plate 2. Christ, detail

Plate 3. The Lamb of God, in the apex of the triumphal arch

Plate 4. Flying angel and medallion with John the Baptist

Plate 5. Moses unlooses his sandals in front of the burning bush

Plate 6. Moses receives the law at the top of Mount Sinai

Plate 7. The Transfiguration, apse mosaic in Sant Apollinare in Classe in Ravenna (549)

Plate 8. Saint Apollinaris in glory, detail

Plate 9. The Incarnation and the Transfiguration, Ottonian manuscript illumination
(eleventh century)

Plate 10. The Transfiguration, icon attributed to Theophane the Greek from the
Cathedral of the Transfiguration in Pereslavl (1403)

Plate 11. Christ, detail

Plate 12. The Transfiguration, from the Church Feast tier in the Annunciation Cathedral, Moscow. By Andrei Rublev (1405)

Plate 13. The Transfiguration, from the Church Feast tier in the Church of the Dormition, Volotovo Polye. Novgorod school (1475–500)

Plate 14. The Ladder of Divine Ascent, icon from the Monastery of Saint Catherine in Sinai (ca. 1150)

Plate 15. Saint Macarios of Egypt, fresco from the Church of the Transfiguration in Novgorod, by Theophane the Greek (1378)

Plate 16. The Transfiguration, by the author

The holy Apollinaris is what he is through his relationship with Christ. He can therefore not be seen isolated from the medallion of the cross. Apollinaris was the first bishop of Ravenna and the only martyr of the city. Through his bishopric he reflects Christ as the shepherd and high priest, and through his martyrdom he imitates the humiliation and subsequent exultation. The outstretched hands symbolize both the praying priest and the suffering martyr. The transfiguration of Christ typifies the deification of man, and Apollinaris manifests the deified man.

The apostle Paul encourages the believers to seek deification (theosis) or transformation into greater likeness with Christ (transfiguration) when he writes that *"we all, with unveiled face, beholding the glory of the Lord, are being changed into his likeness from one degree of glory to another"* (II Cor. 3:18). By placing Apollinaris just under the transfigured Christ, the idea that the martyr is *"changed into his likeness"* as Christ is clearly apparent. Christ is the "Urbild," Apollinaris is the "Abbild."

The relationship between Christ and Apollinaris is also expressed in the relationship between the altar and the grave of the martyr. By placing the martyr's bodily remains under the altar, his sacrifice is tied to the sacrifice of Christ which again is made present through the eucharistic sacrifice. The drama which is described iconographically in the mosaic reflects itself liturgically on the altar. The early Church interpreted martyrdom as a mystical union with Christ. In this way there arose a strong connection between *martyrdom* and *mystery*.[52] As was mentioned before, the Greek word "mystery" is used about the sacramental union of Christ with the believer. By receiving bread and wine which are changed into the body and blood of Christ, man is gradually transformed into that which he is receiving. Both these processes are characterized as transformation or transfiguration — that of going from one state to another — without man's original identity falling away. Just as Christ did not lose his heavenly nature by partaking of human nature, neither does man lose his human nature by partaking of the divine nature.

The two archangels who together with the fruit-bearing palms flank the scene in the apse, visualize the invisible bond between the church in heaven and on earth. Since the earthly liturgy is an icon of its heavenly counterpart, the celebrating priest or bishop becomes an icon of the heav-

52. This idea is from Otto G. von Simson in *Sacred Fortress,* p. 48.

enly high priest, and the deacons who serve by the altar become icons of the archangels Michael and Gabriel.

The archangel Gabriel revealed himself to the high priest Zachariah when, *"according to the custom of the priesthood, it fell to him by lot to enter the temple of the Lord and burn incense. And the whole multitude of the people were praying outside at the hour of incense. And there appeared to him an angel of the Lord standing on the right side of the altar of incense. (. . .) And the angel answered him, "I am Gabriel, who stand in the presence of God"* (Luke 1:9b-11, 19). In Sant Apollinare in Classe this angel is represented at the right side of the altar. In this way the Christian sacrifice of the mass is tied to its Jewish prefiguration and its heavenly archetype. In the Roman liturgy of the mass we find the idea that the sacrificial gifts are carried by angels to the altar of God in heaven.

The four bishops Ecclesius, Severus, Ursus and Ursicinus pose in full liturgical garb beneath their glorified predecessor Apollinaris. This strong episcopal presence demonstrates the importance of the office of the bishop and the hierarchical structure of the Church. Each one has a wreath hanging over his head.

The apostle Peter reminds us of the responsibility and reward that follows the office of the bishop:

> not as domineering over those in our charge, but being examples to the flock. And when the chief Shepherd is manifested you will obtain the unfading crown of glory. (I Pet. 5:3-4)

The Hope of Glory

We have seen that the mosaics in Sant Apollinare in Classe refer to various historical events which are made current through a *liturgical present tense.* In the following discussion we will see that the mosaic points towards an eschatological future. In order to form a better picture of this future, we will begin with an apocryphal text from about the middle of the first century called "The Revelation of Peter."

This text was well known and often quoted by many Church fathers, but the evaluation of its status, in relation to the Canon, varied greatly.

Clement of Alexandria (active about 200) includes the manuscript in an abbreviated review of the canonical texts, Eusebius (active about 325) calls it a fake and without catholic authority, while Methodius of Olympus (active about 300) indirectly refers to the writing as divinely inspired. The revelation of Peter was nevertheless not incorporated into the final Canon.[53] The text begins with all the twelve disciples being together with Jesus on a high mountain. They express the wish to see a glimpse of life after death. There are several indicators which show that this happened after the death and resurrection of Jesus. Two unnamed men appear in glory — here is a clear parallel to Moses and Elijah on Tabor, but the text does not mention anything about the appearance of Jesus being transformed. We get a description of the state of the righteous and the unrighteous in the next world — a vision of heaven and hell which has influenced people's conceptions of the apocalypse throughout the Middle Ages. We find several features similar to the story of the Transfiguration, but with one important difference: namely that the Revelation of Peter emphasizes the eschatological and transcendent more than the historical and dogmatic aspects.

> And furthermore the Lord said: Let us go into the mountain: Let us pray. And going with him, we, the twelve disciples, begged that he would show us one of our brethren, the righteous who are gone forth out of the world, in order that we might see of what manner of form they are. (. . .) And as we prayed, suddenly there appeared two men standing before the Lord towards the East, on whom we were not able to look; for there came forth from their countenance a ray as of the sun, and their raiment was shining, such as eye of men never saw; for no mouth is able to express or heart to conceive the glory with which they were endued, and the beauty of their appearance (. . .), and I am utterly unable to express their beauty. (. . .)
>
> And I approached the Lord and said: Who are these? He saith to me: These are your brethren the righteous, whose forms ye desired to see. And I said to him: And where are all the righteous ones and what is the æon in which they are and have this glory?

53. From the introduction to *The Apocalypse of Peter,* The Ante-Nicene Fathers, Volume X, p. 145.

And the Lord showed me a very great country outside of this world, exceeding bright with light, and the air there lighted with the rays of the sun, and the earth itself blooming with unfading flowers and full of spices and plants, fair-flowering and incorruptible and bearing blessed fruit.

And so great was the perfume that it was borne thence even unto us. And the dwellers in that place were clad in the raiment of shining angels and their raiment was like unto their country; and angels hovered about them there. And the glory of the dwellers there were equal, and with one voice they sang praises alternately to the Lord God, rejoicing in that place. The Lord saith to us: This is the place of your high-priests, the righteous men.[54]

The many references to the revelation of Peter in early patristic literature give a reasonable basis for belief that its content was known among those responsible for the decoration of Sant Apollinare in Classe, but a definite connection has never been established.

The synoptic gospels tell of the transfiguration of Jesus as a passing episode in this life, while the vision of paradise in the Revelation of Peter describes a lasting state in the next life. Both sources describe a supernatural light which makes a deep impression on the disciples. That the landscape and plants also were effected by the light is most clearly expressed in the apocryphal text. The face, clothes, air, plants, even the earth itself is irradiated with an energy of light which made a divine presence visible. We see into an existence *"outside of this world, exceeding bright with light"* where the air is *"lighted with the rays of the sun."* The mosaic's glowing gold sky and transparent clouds illustrate how the uncreated light transfigures all it touches.

The text tells further that *"the earth itself (was) blooming with unfading flowers and full of spices and plants, fair-flowering and incorruptible and bearing blessed fruit."* Here it talks about a landscape with a supernatural nature. Words like *"unfading, incorruptible and blessed"* express something transcendent as opposed to the experiences of this life. The known laws of nature are abolished and replaced with ones that are new and unknown. The

54. *The Apocalypse of Peter,* The Ante-Nicene Fathers, Volume X, p. 145.

uncreated light pervades created matter and causes it to radiate from within. The mosaic's idealized landscape is similar to "radiant" nature described in the text.

Towards the end of the quote Jesus says that *"This is the place of your high-priests, the righteous men."* "The righteous high-priest" — Bishop Apollinaris — stands praying, as though he is officiating at the altar in a heavenly garden. As mentioned above, Apollinaris is represented by his relics under the altar and by his icon in the mosaic. The relics are testimonies of a radical imitation of Christ whilst simultaneously pointing towards *"the resurrection of the body and eternal life,"*[55] while the icon of Apollinaris refers to the attainment of perfection after the resurrection. This state is marked by the uncreated light which radiates from the face of Christ on Tabor and can be explained by an unceasing transfiguration where *"God shall be all in all"* (I Cor. 15:28). In the mosaic we see how men, animals, plants and minerals reveal themselves in eschatological glory. Just as the whole creation at one point in the past experienced the consequences of the fall, so also the whole creation at one point in the future will experience the consequences of the Incarnation. The apostle Paul expounds upon this vision of the future when he says:

> For the creation waits with eager longing for the revealing of the sons of God (. . .) because the creation itself will be set free from its bondage to decay and obtain the glorious liberty of the children of God. (Rom. 8:19, 21)

In the mosaic of Sant Apollinare in Classe the eschatological consequence of the incarnation is visualized. We see a deified man in a transfigured cosmos.

Descent, Ascent and Second Coming

We have seen how the Incarnation is a prerequisite for the Transfiguration and how the event of God descending and being made man is the starting point for man's ascent and deification.

---

55. From the Apostolic creed.

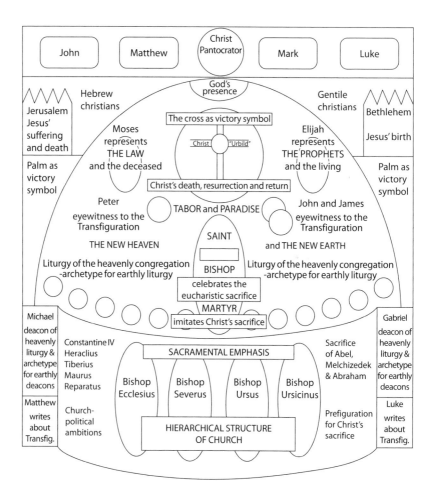

John Matthew Christ Pantocrator Mark Luke

God's presence

Jerusalem
Jesus' suffering and death

Hebrew christians

The cross as victory symbol

Christ   "Urbild"

Moses represents THE LAW and the deceased

Christ's death, resurrection and return

Gentile christians

Elijah represents THE PROPHETS and the living

Bethlehem

Jesus' birth

Palm as victory symbol

Peter eyewitness to the Transfiguration

TABOR and PARADISE

John and James eyewitness to the Transfiguration

Palm as victory symbol

THE NEW HEAVEN

SAINT

and THE NEW EARTH

Liturgy of the heavenly congregation -archetype for earthly liturgy

BISHOP celebrates the eucharistic sacrifice

MARTYR imitates Christ's sacrifice

Liturgy of the heavenly congregation -archetype for earthly liturgy

Michael deacon of heavenly liturgy & archetype for earthly deacons

Constantine IV
Heraclius
Tiberius
Maurus
Reparatus

SACRAMENTAL EMPHASIS

Bishop Ecclesius

Bishop Severus

Bishop Ursus

Bishop Ursicinus

Sacrifice of Abel, Melchizedek & Abraham

Gabriel deacon of heavenly liturgy & archetype for earthly deacons

Matthew writes about Transfig.

Church-political ambitions

HIERARCHICAL STRUCTURE OF CHURCH

Prefiguration for Christ's sacrifice

Luke writes about Transfig.

The life of Jesus can be characterized as a series of different descents and ascents. He descended from heaven by his birth, he descended into the river Jordan at his baptism, he ascended up to Tabor at his transfiguration, he was lifted up on the cross and taken down from the cross, he was laid in a grave, he descended into hell, he arose from the grave and ascended into heaven. These events occur between the great descent, which is the birth of Jesus, and the great ascent, which is his ascension into heaven. Jesus' own remark that *"No one has ascended into heaven but he who descended from heaven"* (John 3:13) contains therefore a christological summary.

Through the great descent, God became man, by the great ascent, human nature is brought back to God since Jesus, who ascended into heaven, is both true God and true man. This "katabasis — anabasis" pattern also spans into the future through the anticipation of the second coming of Christ. Along with the ascension of Jesus it was preached that *"This Jesus, who was taken up from you into heaven, will come in the same way as you saw him go into heaven"* (Acts 1:11).

The fact that the mosaic is placed in the apse of a church whose axis is east-west emphasizes here a deeper connection between location and meaning. The convention requiring a church to be oriented in such a way that the apse faces east comes from the anticipation that Christ will come again from there where the sun rises. In another version of the Revelation of Peter where the second coming of Christ is talked about, Jesus says, *"The cross shall go in front of me when I come in glory. And I shall shine seven times stronger than the sun."*[56] The cross with the face of Christ in the centre of the sun-medallion can be seen as an iconographical illustration of this prophecy.

Based upon the interpretation we have given of the mosaic in Sant Apollinare in Classe, we can establish the model on page 82.

56. Quoted from Gertrud Schiller, *Ikonographie der Christlicher Kunst* I, p. 156.

The Transfiguration, with Reference to
Theophane the Greek's Transfiguration Icon

From Theology to Anthropology

The iconographical starting point for further reflections will be the Russian Transfiguration icon attributed to Theophane the Greek. Since this icon is dated from the beginning of the thirteenth century, we have a long and comprehensive interpretive tradition through which to view the motif. We will make use of both literary and iconographical sources in order to penetrate the meaning of the motif.

Up until now we have concentrated mainly on the theological and christological aspects of the Transfiguration, on what the episode at Tabor indicates about God and Christ. In the following section we will look more closely at the anthropological side, what the story says about man.

In the interpretation of the Sinai mosaic, the burning bush and the light from the transfigured Christ were defined as God's uncreated energies in the form of fire and light. Theophanies in the Old and in the New Testament tell how God in various ways discloses who he is, how he allows his being to "shine through" the ontological and moral abyss between himself, the uncreated and holy God, and created and sinful man. We shall see how the accentuation of the uncreated light in this icon actualizes what consequences the Transfiguration has towards understanding man, not as autonomous, but as a primarily God-related being.

The source for the uncreated light is God's unattainable essence. But what happens at the other end of the ray of light? What happens when man and creation in general come within the field of energy of the uncreated light? It is natural to seek the answers to these questions here because the Orthodox church discussed such problems conciliarly about fifty years before Theophane the Greek painted his Transfiguration icon.[57] Because the art of the icon should reflect current doctrine and thereby express orthodoxy visually, the icon motivates us to study the effects of the light of Tabor.[58] Another

---

57. See John Meyendorff, *A Study of Gregory Palamas*, from p. 42.

58. With this it is not suggested that there is a direct cause and effect relationship between the theological debate in Byzantium during 1330 and 1350 (namely the debate of

feature characteristic of this icon and which also motivates our research is the two caves in the mountain side between Christ and the disciples. By showing these caves as hermit cells in a wild and desolate landscape, we are reminded of the spiritual inheritance from the desert fathers. The organized monastic life which developed over the years grew from the spontaneous spirituality which these early hermits represented. It is within these contemplative traditions we must search in order to gain understanding of the anthropological aspect of the Transfiguration.

The Image and the Likeness of God

Attack is grounds for defense. Throughout the fourteenth century it is the attack on a monastic spirituality known as Hesychasm which actualizes the defense of the current Byzantine anthropology. At this time we see the contours of the dawning Renaissance in the West. It was more and more common to interpret existence from an anthropocentric world view inspired by pre-christian, antique ideals. In the East on the other hand, the Greeks enunciate a clear distance from their own Hellenistic inheritance. Instead of reaching back into platonistic dualism, they develop further the medieval theocentric view of man. Before we delve further into the details of Hesychasm, we will briefly summarize its anthropological basis. We begin at the beginning:

> Then God said: "Let us make man in our image, in our likeness."
> (Gen. 1:26)

The expression "created in the image of God" indicates the status of man, what man is, while the expression "created in the likeness of God" indicates the potential of man, what man can be. The first is a gift, the second is a challenge. God creates man with a free will and with the ability to love. Freedom is a prerequisite for love. The paradoxical situation of man

---

Hesychasm which ended with victory for the Hesychasts and which will be discussed later) and Theophane the Greek's Transfiguration icon, yet Hesychasm was strongly represented in Russia, both as a political and monastic movement during the time Theophane the Greek was active. See Jostein Børtnes, *Visions of Glory,* from p. 109.

is that he is both dependent and free. He is fundamentally dependent on God because he is created, and he is fundamentally free in relation to God because he is created in the image of God. It was not that God had to create man, but that he wanted to. Man is a result of the free will of God. The relationship between the creator and his highest creation is a relationship between persons. Man stands free to develop or turn against this relationship.

By separating free will from love of God, man alienates himself from his divine origin. Because the divine image is constitutive for man, the fall brings about a darkening of the image, not its total destruction. Man remained man after the fall, but he has received a basic flaw which cannot be repaired without divine intervention.

This intervention happens at the Incarnation, and the renewing effect of the Incarnation is given to man as a gift through baptism. Deification of man, which is a dialogue between the free will of man and the uncreated grace of God, has a sacramental foundation. Just as conception occurs before growth, the sacrament comes before asceticism. Diadochos of Photiki (ca. 400–ca. 486) explains the restoration of fallen man as a combination of rebirth and deification:

> Divine grace confers on us two gifts through the baptism of regeneration. (. . .) The first gift is given to us at once, when grace renews us in the actual waters of baptism and cleanses all the lineaments of our soul, that is, the image of God in us, by washing away every stain of sin. The second — our likeness to God — requires our cooperation.[59]

The reborn man is like an unfinished work of art where *"grace is beginning to paint the divine likeness over the divine image in us."*[60] Macarios of Egypt (ca. 300–390) deals as well with how man can reclaim likeness with God when he says:

---

59. Diadochos of Photiki, *Spiritual Knowledge and Discrimination*, §89, *The Philokalia*, Volume I, p. 288.
60. Loc. cit., p. 248.

> But above all the eyes of the soul must be fixed on Christ, who, like a
> good painter, paints in those who believe in him and constantly be-
> hold him a portrait of the heavenly man.[61]

Macarios reasons that the light that transfigured Christ at Tabor is the same
light which transforms man into the likeness of God. The uncreated light is
itself the substance with which Christ paints in order to bring out the true
likeness with *"the heavenly man."* Christ is both painter and model.

Theosis as the Transfiguration of Man

Just as the ascension of Jesus was a physical ascent to heaven, the deification
of man (theosis) is a spitirual ascent to heaven. The idea of the deification of
man as a spiritual ascent is clearly seen in an icon from Sinai, dated from the
last half of the twelfth century (plate 12). We see a ladder diagonally span-
ning from earth into heaven. The ladder has thirty steps. A row of monks
climb up the ladder; several fall off in the process because they are drawn
down by small, black demons. *"For demons are the friends of sin."*[62] The
monks are involved in a spiritual battle which includes release from vices
and development of virtues. By placing the ladder between groups of angels
and demons, the painter has illustrated that the battle rages both in man's
consciousness and in the spiritual world. Christ appears in a half-circle in
the upper right corner and receives those who have withstood the demonic
undertow. The inscriptions tell that the two men at the top of the ladder are
John Climacus and a certain Anthony. The latter clothed in the robe of a
bishop is somewhat larger than the anonymous monks who follow from behind.

John Climacus (ca. 579–ca. 649) lived as a hermit in a cave for forty
years in the mountains outside the monastery of Saint Catherine in Sinai.
At one time he was the abbot of the monastery. The thirty steps on the ladder correspond to the thirty virtues with their opposite vices which John

---

61. Macarios of Egypt, "Homily 34, 1," quoted after Vladimir Lossky, *Vision of God,*
p. 115.

62. Athanasios av Alexandria, *Antonios liv,* 7, p. 50.

Climacus classifies in the book *The Ladder of Divine Ascent*. Here John Climacus poses a question which gives a fitting description of the spiritual drama illustrated by the icon:

> There is one thing which never ceases to amaze me. Why is it that when we have Almighty God, the angels, and the saints to help us toward virtue, and when only the devil is against us, we still incline so readily to the passions?[63]

We see how *"Almighty God, the angels, and saints help us towards virtue,"* but that many of the monks nevertheless *"incline so readily to the passions."* And the devil himself is represented as a gaping maw who devours a monk directly beneath the ladder. John Climacus continues:

> how is it as the great Gregory puts it, that I am the image of God, yet mingled with clay? Is it not a fact that a creature of God that has strayed from its created nature will continuously try to return to its original condition? Indeed everyone should struggle to raise his clay, so to speak, to a place on the throne of God.[64]

The monks on the ladder are about to *"return to their original condition."* They strive to regain the likeness with God which Adam had before the fall. The "theosis" of man can be explained as a step-by-step transfiguration where man is transformed into greater likeness with God through continually greater participation in the divine nature.

Mysticism of Intellect and Mysticism of Experience

The two caves in Theophane the Greek's Transfiguration icon, which we here have called hermit cells, direct our thoughts towards the ascetic and contemplative practice which the desert fathers and their monastic followers exercised. The hermit cell is a place for material renunciation and spiri-

---

63. John Climacus, *The Ladder of Divine Ascent,* Step 26, On Discernment, p. 223.
64. Loc. cit. p. 248.

tual growth. Outside impulses are reduced to a minimum such that the monk cannot avoid being confronted with his own self. Increasing self-insight gives deeper acknowledgement of his own sins and contributes towards greater humility. According to John Climacus this basic virtue *"is a God-given protection against seeing our own achievements. (. . .) You will know that you have this holy gift within you,"* this ascetic teacher continues, *"(. . .) when you experience an abundance of unspeakable light together with an indescribable love of prayer."*[65]

The interior of the mountain is dark; only the entrance is defined by a strong light. The most credible interpretation is that this darkness is a lack of light, and that those who are in "the dark" live in a state of ignorance.[66] But we shall turn this interpretation around and rather view the darkness as an expression of the divine darkness which the mystic is cast into when seeking union with God. The caves are an iconographical feature apropos to apophatic theology. It was this divine darkness which surrounded Moses on Sinai. On Tabor the light from the transfigured Christ was so strong that the disciples became blinded. It was, in other words, so bright that their vision was darkened. That the disciples experienced this light as overwhelming and incomprehensible is signified by their poses. They twist themselves into a ball and hold their hands in front of their faces. The darkness symbolizes both the contemplative life's goal defined as mystical union with God, and the realization that this happens independently of intellectual insight. The mystic understands that he cannot understand what he experiences.

The caves on the Transfiguration icon inspire us to seek the source of the mystical theology of the Eastern Church. We will consider two different currents within the monastic milieu of Egypt in the fourth century

---

65. John Climacus, *The Ladder of Divine Ascent,* Step 24, On Meekness, Simplicity, Guilelessness and Wickedness, p. 223.

66. We might think of Plato's parable of the cave man who sits with his back towards the light and mistakes the shadows on the wall for the actual form. According to the platonic world view, the shadows are the same as the illusive world of the senses, while the light outside the cave is the real world, namely the world of ideas. Because Christ manifested his divine nature on Tabor, he revealed his real nature as true God and true man. Yet it is risky, if not directly misguided, to use platonic terms to interpret icons since the view of matter within Platonism and Christianity stands diametrically opposed to each other. The transfiguration does not entail dematerialization, but illumination of the created. And the created is absolutely real and, as it says in Genesis 1, "good."

which can be called "intellectual mysticism" and "mysticism of experience." The intellectual mysticism is here represented by Evagrios of Pontos (ca. 345–399) and the mysticism of experience by Macarios of Egypt (ca. 300–390).[67] The intellectual mysticism and the mysticism of experience can be seen as the extremes of spirituality which prevailed in Byzantine and, later, Slavonic regions. The interchange between formulated experience and experience, between doctrine and lived life, results in a theology where mysticism and the development of dogma influence each other.

Evagrios can be viewed as holding a speculative, platonized theology, the root of which is found in Alexandria. He considers himself a disciple of the Cappadocian fathers — Basil the Great, Gregory of Nyssa and Gregory Nazianzus. Towards the end of his life he settles among hermits in the Egyptian desert. He builds primarily upon the thoughts of Origen in his emphasis on the intellect (nous) as the place where man meets God. The word "nous" is translated both as intellect, spirit and mind. In patristic literature the intellect is not man's ability to reason, but his deepest "spiritual sense" or "contemplative organ" which in its purest form can acknowledge divine truths.[68] Macarios advocates a more pragmatic spirituality where the sayings and experiences of the desert fathers are used as examples for the spiritual life. He considers the heart (cardia) as the seat of man's personality and thereby contributes to the establishment of the Jesus-prayer practice. Macarios calls the intellect "the eye of the heart." Both of these currents can, in overdeveloped versions, turn into heresies which result in condemnation. The intellectual mysticism can lead to over-accentuation on the intellect as man's essential centre and the place where man is met by the divine.[69] The mysticism of experience can emphasize the affective aspect of man's relationship with God so much that the church as an institution and the sacramental and liturgical life can be seen as unnecessary (Messalianism). Common for both these blind alleys is that a one-sided anthropology

67. It is unknown if the ascetic texts called "The Homilies of Macarios" really were written by Macarios of Egypt, but the texts which bear his name have in many cases had a decisive influence on and are often quoted in Greek patristic literature.

68. From the glossary in *The Philokalia*, Volume I, p. 362.

69. At the Council of Constantinople in 553, Evagrios and Origen were condemned for the more speculative aspects of their theology. Yet Evagrios' teaching on the contemplative life was highly respected within the monastic tradition.

leads to a distorted theology which in its turn has negative consequences for ecclesiology.

Throughout the fifth century valuable psychological insights from these currents were channeled into the monastic milieu by Diadochos of Photici (ca. 400–ca. 486). Diadochos takes advantage of both Evagrios and Macarios in his advice for the spiritual life and envisages a synthesis where "nous" and "cardia" are integrated parts of the anthropology. As with Evagrios, Diadochos sees the fall as a fatal fragmentation of the will and the intellect. The continual stream of thoughts thwarts the mind's pure contemplation of God and activates the passions such that man falls into sin. Evagrios defines prayers as "the shedding of thoughts."[70] Here Diadochos comes with advice on the use of short concentrated prayers (monologia) which help to discipline the restless thoughts. Prayer is both "light for the intellect" and "warmth for the heart."[71] A perpetual inner remembrance of God's presence (mneme Theou) satisfies the need the mind has for activity while simultaneously collecting the thoughts.

John Climacus builds upon the inheritance from Diadochos by developing a balanced combination of the practical teachings of Evagrios on the virtues and vices and Macarios' emphasis on direct personal experience. The last step on the ladder to heaven of John Climacus is love. As we have seen with Gregory of Nyssa, development of the virtues is not limited to this life. The ladder represents an unending ascent towards God, because *there is no boundary to virtue (. . .), and if it is true that love never fails* [I Cor. 13:8] *(. . .), then love has no boundary, and both in the present and in the future age we will never cease to progress in it, as we add light to light.*"[72]

The Transfiguration of the Body

As mentioned in the chapter on the Incarnation, man is a psychophysical entity. Man is created in the image of God, both with body, soul, and spirit.

70. Evagrios the Solitary, "On Prayer" §71, *The Philokalia,* Vol. I, p. 64.
71. Diadochos of Photiki, *Spiritual Knowledge and Discrimination,* 6 59, *The Philokalia,* Vol. I, p. 270.
72. John Climacus, *The Ladder of Divine Ascent,* Step 26, On Discernment, pp. 250-251.

The dualistic tendency of juxtaposing the spiritual and the material, or to see deification as a form of dematerialization, does not correspond with the conviction that matter is willed by God and *"very good."*[73] Cyril of Jerusalem (315–386) emphasizes man's unique position in relation to the rest of creation when he says that God *"called all creation good, but only man was made in his image. The sun came into existence by a command, but man was fashioned by God's own divine hands."*[74]

The most important arguments for looking positively at matter (and in this connection man's physical body) is: that man, who is created in the image of God, has a body; that God himself received a body through the Incarnation; that God's sacramental self-communication is through material elements such as bread and wine (the body and blood of Christ); that the resurrection of Christ was a bodily resurrection; and the promise that mortal man will also resurrect bodily. Macarios of Egypt understands the deification of man as an anticipation of the resurrection:

> For what the soul has now stored up within, shall then be revealed and displayed outwardly in the body. (. . .) At the day of resurrection the glory of the Holy Spirit comes out from within, decking and covering the bodies of the saints (. . .) the glory which they had before, but hidden within their souls. What a man has now, the same then comes forth externally in the body. (. . .) Their bodies shall be glorified through the unspeakable light which even now is within them (. . .) that is, the power of the Holy Spirit.[75]

We have seen that the Transfiguration is a prefiguration for the resurrection. On Tabor the appearance of Christ changed so that *"his face shone like the sun, and his garment became white as light"* (Matt. 17:2). The transfiguration had a physical and thereby perceptible effect. The divine identity

---

73. In contrast to the angels, man is an incarnated being. An angel is a created, spiritual being without a body. Man is a created, spiritual being with a body. Gregory of Nyssa, John of Damascus and others claim that man stands higher than the angels precisely because he has a body.

74. Quoted after John of Damascus, *On the Divine Images,* p. 102.

75. Macarios of Egypt, "Homily 5," quoted after Kallistos Ware, *The Transfiguration of the Body,* p. 32.

of Christ, which normally was hidden from the disciples, appeared now *"outwardly in the body."* On Sinai Moses drew so near the source of the uncreated radiance that he was completely permeated by it. It is said that *"Moses did not know that the skin of his face shone because he had been talking with God"* (Exod. 34:29). Moses received a fortaste of the perfect life in the immediate presence of God. According to Paul, however, it is not until the age to come that he will *"change our lowly body to be like his glorious body"* (Phil. 3:21).

That which affects the soul will also affect the body. Macarios elaborates on this simple psychosomatic principle in order to explain the underlying dynamics of the resurrection. The same dynamics also apply in more rare instances of visible transfiguration of the human body. Such instances tell of the sacred capacity of the body and of the will of man to let himself be cleansed and enlightened by the uncreated light. Man is mortal and the body transient, but death and transience are a result of the fall and not what was originally natural. Therefore Christ, "the heavenly man," can say about himself, *"No one takes my life from me, but I lay it down of my own accord"* (John 10:18). In another passage it is written that *"it was not possible for him to be held in the power of death"* (Acts 2:24).

John Climacus emphasizes that the transformation into a greater likeness to God is not only an inner phenomenon of the soul, but also includes the body. For, he says, *"a man flooded with the love of God reveals in his body, as if in a mirror, the splendor of his soul, a glory like that of Moses when he came face to face with God."*[76] In his extensive reflections over what characterizes a holy life, he often refers to the body: *"I do not think anyone should be classed as a saint until he has made holy his body, if indeed that is possible."*[77] Maximos Confessor (580-662) explains likewise that *"the body is deified along with the soul through its own corresponding participation in the process of deification. Thus God alone is made manifest through the soul and the body, since their natural properties have been overcome by the superabundance of his glory."*[78] It is particularly among the ascetic Desert Fathers and those of like mind that we

76. John Climacus, *The Ladder of Divine Ascent,* Step 30, On Faith, Hope and Love, p. 288.

77. Ibid., Step 15, On Chastity, p. 178.

78. Maximos Confessor, *Two Hundred Texts on Theology and the Incarnate Dispensation of the Son of God,* Second Century, §88, *The Philokalia,* Volume II, p. 160.

find examples of such an external manifestation of *"the unspeakable light which even now is within them."* These transfigurations of the saints refer therefore both to man's original natural state before the fall and to man's glorified state after the resurrection. Maximos has this eschatological perspective in mind when he says that God is *"secretly pre-delineating in them the features of his future advent as if in an icon."*[79] In the time between these events God partook of human nature such that man could partake of divine nature. According to this theocentric anthropology the transfiguration of man is a visible expression for partaking of divine nature. "Theosis" does not imply that the differences between the divine and the human are erased. On the contrary, greater likeness with God will make man more human since the deified man has developed his God-given potential. Man will always be created and God will always be uncreated. Iron which is heated by fire is still iron, but is different from cold iron in that it can be formed.[80]

The following are four examples of visual transfiguration of the body among the Desert Fathers. These instances will be commented upon later.

> On another Desert father St. Pambo, it is said; God so glorified him that no one could look at his face, because of the glory which his face had. (. . .) Just as Moses received the image of the glory of Adam, when his face was glorified, so the face of Abba Pambo shone like lightning, and he was as a king seated on his throne.[81]

> There came to the abbot Joseph the abbot Lot, and said to him, "Father, according to my strength I keep a modest rule of prayer, fasting, meditation and quiet, and according to my strength I purge my imagination: what more must I do?" The old man, rising, held up his hands against the sky, and his fingers became like ten torches of fire, and he said, "If thou wilt, thou shalt be made wholly a flame."[82]

---

79. Ibid., 28, p. 144.

80. This metaphor is used by John of Damascus: "They (the holy) are truly called gods, not by nature, but by adoption, just as red-hot iron is called fiery, not by its adoption, but because it participates in the action of the fire." Quoted from *On the Divine Images,* III, 33, p. 84.

81. Quoted from Kallistos Ware, "The Transfiguration of the Body," p. 21.

82. Quoted after Helen Waddell, *The Desert Fathers,* p. 157.

A brother went to the cell of abbot Arsenius in Scete, and looked through the window, and saw the old man as it were one flame: now, the brother was worthy to look upon such things. And after he had knocked, the old man came out, and saw the brother as one amazed, and said to him, "Hast thou seen aught?" And he answered, "No." And he talked with him, and sent him away.[83]

This same abbot Sosois sitting in his cell would ever have his door closed. But it was told of him how in the day of his sleeping, when the Fathers were sitting around him, his face shone like the sun, and he said to them, "Look, the abbot Anthony comes."[84] And after a little while, he said again to them, "Look, the company of the prophets comes." And again his fase shone brighter, and he said, "Look, the company of the apostles comes." And his face shone with a double glory, and lo, he seemed as though he spoke with others. And the old men entreated him, saying, "With whom art thou speaking, Father?" And he said to them, "Behold, the angels came to take me, and I asked that I might be left a little while to repent." The old men said to him, "Thou hast no need of repentance, Father." But he said to them, "Verily I know not if I have clutched at the very beginning of repentance." And they all knew that he was made perfect. And again of a sudden his face was as the sun, and they all were in dread. And he said to them, "Look, behold the Lord cometh, saying, 'Bring me my chosen from the desert.'" And straightway he gave up the ghost. And there came as it might be lightning, and all the place was filled with sweetness.[85]

---

83. Ibid., p. 177.

84. The text here refers to Anthony the Great (250-356), often called "the father of monastic life."

85. Helen Waddell, *The Desert Fathers,* pp. 180-181.

Hesychasm[86]

Of the Greek church fathers, Gregory Palamas (1296-1359) is probably the one who has reflected most deeply over the relationship between the uncreated light and created matter. As John of Damascus gave the icon theological legitimacy in the eighth century, Gregory of Palamas gave Hesychasm theological legitimacy in the fourteenth century. In both instances it was the attack on a formerly established tradition in the Church which predicated the need for defining a precise theological basis for this tradition. Both John of Damascus and Gregory Palamas would in time receive conciliar support for their theology.

Hesychasm is a psychophysical method of prayer which promotes a lasting, inner communion with God. By combining a short formula of prayer with breathing in and out, the divine presence is integrated into the rhythm of the body. The praying person concentrates all his attention towards the heart and recites: "Lord Jesus Christ, Son of God, have mercy on me, a sinner."[87] Such a contemplative practice is an immediate and concrete interpretation of the apostolic admonition to "pray without ceasing" (I Thess. 5:17). The spirituality of Hesychasm can be traced back to the Desert Fathers, but the method itself was presented in a more systematic form at the turn of the thirteenth century. An important name to mention here is Gregory of Sinai (ca. 1265–1346), but we also find references to hesychastic prayer in earlier spiritual writings such as that of Diadochos of Photiki (ca. 400–ca. 486), John Climacus (ca. 579–ca. 649) and Symeon the New Theologian (949-1022).

Diadochos emphasizes that the recitation of the holy name has a disciplining effect on the intellect and a cleansing influence on the soul:

> Let the intellect continually concentrate on these words within its
> inner shrine with such intensity that it is not turned aside to any

---

86. The term "hesychia" etymologically means peace, concentration, being still. The title "hesychast" is used early as a synonym for hermit, a monk who lives alone, as opposed to a cenobite, a monk who lives in a monastic fellowship. Here it refers to one who adheres to the particular monastic spirituality "hesychasm" which Gregory Palamas defends.

87. This formula is a classic version of the so-called Jesus Prayer and is taken from the pleading of the blind beggar: "Jesus, son of David, have mercy on me" (Luke 18:38) and the humble publican: "God, be merciful to me, a sinner" (Luke 18:13).

mental images. Those who meditate unceasingly upon this glorious and holy name in the depth of their heart can sometimes see the light of their own intellect. For when the mind is closely concentrated upon this name, then we grow fully conscious that the name is burning up all the filth which covers the surface of the soul; for it is written: "Our God is a consuming fire."[88]

John Climacus advises practicing the Jesus-prayer as a help for continual inner attentiveness and as a defense against temptations and distractions:

Let the remembrance of Jesus be present with your every breath. Then indeed you will appreciate the value of stillness (hesychia).[89]

Symeon the New Theologian tells of two ecstatic experiences of light in connection with hesychastic prayer. These visions of light have several similarities with the transfiguration the disciples witnessed at Tabor and the enrapturement Paul experienced, but which he refrained from describing further (II Cor. 12:1-5). Because of their strong personal character, these descriptions are unique within Byzantine, ascetic literature:

One day, as he stood and recited, "God, have mercy upon me, a sinner," uttering it with his mind rather than his mouth, suddenly a flood of divine radiance appeared from above and filled all the room. As this happened the young man lost all awareness (of his surroundings) and forgot that he was in a house or that he was under a roof. He saw nothing but light all around him and did not know if he was standing on the ground. (. . .) Instead, he was wholly in the presence of immaterial light and seemed to himself to have turned into light. Oblivious of all the world he was filled with tears and ineffable joy and gladness.[90]

I fell prostrate to the ground, and at once I saw, and behold, a great light was immaterially shining on me and seized hold of my whole

88. Diadochos of Photiki, *Spiritual Knowledge and Discrimination*, §59, *The Philokalia*, Vol. I, p. 270.
89. John Climacus, *The Ladder of Divine Ascent*, Step 27, On Stillness, p. 270.
90. Symeon the New Theologian, *The Discourses*, pp. 245-246.

mind and soul, so that I was struck with amazement at the unexpected marvel and I was, as it were, in ecstacy. Moreover I forgot the place where I stood, who I was, and where, and could only cry out, "Lord, have mercy," so that when I came to myself I discovered that I was reciting this. "But Father," said he, "who it was that was speaking, and who moved my tongue, I do not know — only God knows." "Whether I was in the body, or outside the body" [II Cor. 12:2-3], I conversed with this Light. The Light itself knows it; it scattered whatever mist there was in my soul and cast out every earthly care. It expelled from me all material denseness and bodily heaviness that made my members to be sluggish and numb. What an awesome marvel! It so invigorated and strengthened my limbs and muscles, which had been faint through great weariness, that it seemed to me as though I was stripping myself of the garment of corruption. Besides, there was poured into my soul in unutterable fashion a great spiritual joy and perception and a sweetness surpassing every taste of visible objects, together with a freedom and forgetfulness of all thoughts pertaining to this life. In a marvelous way there was granted to me and revealed to me the manner of the departure from this present life. Thus all the perceptions of my mind and my soul were wholly concentrated on the ineffable joy of that Light.[91]

Criticism and Defense of Hesychasm

The Hesychasts are not criticized for their spiritual eagerness, but for their insistence that the body, together with soul and spirit, takes part in divine nature. Moreover, they were unjustly blamed for sympathizing with the Messalians — a previously banned sect which claimed that the essence of God could be contemplated with the physical eye.[92] This very serious cri-

---

91. Symeon the New Theologian, ibid., pp. 200-201.

92. The Messalians, whose western counterpart are the Kathars, are strongly dualistic in their understanding of the world and man. They are critical of the Church as an institution and put little emphasis on the sacraments. Since the Hesychasts are not antisacramental, Barlaam uses the term "Material Messalianism" when he speaks against the psychophysical prayer practice of the Hesychasts.

tique forced the Hesychasts to literally creep out of their caves in order to defend their own spirituality. Gregory Palamas unwillingly broke off his contemplative life on Mt. Athos and engaged in a comprehensive theological debate with the Greek-Italian monk and philosopher Barlaam of Calabria (ca. 1290–1348).[93] A recurring theme in this debate is precisely that of the divergent interpretations of the theological and anthropological aspects of the Transfiguration.

Barlaam has a rationalistic attitude inspired by Neoplatonistic thought. God reveals himself from outside of our universe, through Scripture and Tradition, and imparts himself to the intellect (nous). Deeper insight into the divine mystery is not possible to achieve in this life. Gregory claims that God reveals himself from within, through direct giving of his presence in the heart (cardia), and that knowledge of God (gnosis) cannot be separated from deification (theosis). "Knowledge is not the light! Rather, it is the light which is knowledge,"[94] says Symeon the New Theologian. This way of speaking reflects a conviction that true knowledge of God can be won only through experience. The type of knowledge the mystic seeks is more existential than intellectual. Here the Hesychastic method of prayer comes in as an aid for making the monk more open to the uncreated grace.

When Gregory calls the grace of God uncreated, it is to emphasize that man is dependent on a supernatural initiative from outside this finite world if he is to gain knowledge of and likeness to his divine origin. It is a matter of an active appropriation of this uncreated grace. The Hesychasts advocate an anthropology where man has the ability to transcend himself, an ability which springs from being created in the image of God.

Gregory quotes Macarios of Egypt when he argues that it is the heart, not the intellect, which makes up the spiritual centre of the personality:

> The heart directs the entire organism, and when grace gains possession of the heart, it reigns over all the thoughts and all the members;

93. Barlaam belongs to the Greek Orthodox minority of Calabria in southern Italy. According to Kallistos Ware, the controversy of Hesychasm is not an expression of disagreement between Greek and Latin theologians, as it is often portrayed, but rather an internal discussion between Greek theologians on how Dionysius the Areopagite should be interpreted. See Kallistos Ware, "Studies of Spirituality," p. 249.

94. Symeon the New Theologian, *The Discourses,* p. 301.

for it is there, in the heart, that the mind and all the thoughts of the soul have their seat. (. . .) Macarios immediately goes on to say, "It is there one must look to see if grace has inscribed the laws of the Spirit." Where but in the heart, the controlling organ, the throne of grace, are the mind and all the thoughts of the soul to be found? Can you not see, then, how essential it is that those who have determined to pay attention to themselves in inner quiet should gather together the mind and enclose it in the body, and especially in that "body" most interior to the body, which we call the heart?[95]

The Hesychasts hear that they have their "soul in their navel." This polemic expression refers to the practice of focusing on the stomach in order to achieve greater concentration in prayer. The objective of this method is to bring the mind down to the heart so that the entire man, a combination of body, soul and spirit, can be lifted towards God. According to Gregory, *"it is not out of place to teach people, especially beginners, that they should look at themselves, and introduce their own mind within themselves through control of breathing. (. . .) for those newly approaching this struggle find that their mind, when recollected, continually becomes dispersed again. It is thus necessary for such people constantly to bring it back once more; but in their inexperience, they fail to grasp that nothing in the world is in fact more difficult to contemplate and more mobile and shifting than the mind."*[96] The ironic tendency in Barlaam's critique exposes a generally negative understanding of the body and the material world. In connection with the christological debate, during the iconoclastic period and under the attack on Hesychasm, the relationship between spirit and matter is a recurring problem. Barlaam tends towards Origen's theories of the body by claiming that the body is a hindrance to man's spiritual development.[97] Gregory opposes even the premises for this understanding of the body:

95. Gregory Palamas, *The Triads,* I.ii.1, p. 41.
96. Ibid., I.ii.7, p. 45.
97. "The Fall" for Origen entails a fall into the material. Therefore spiritualization is understood as dematerialization. The mind must be freed from the body in order to achieve the goal of contemplation. Within such a spirituality there is thus little room for the sacraments.

How can it be that God at the beginning caused the mind to inhabit the body? Did even he do ill? Rather, brother, such views befit the heretics, who claim that the body is an evil thing, a fabrication of the Wicked One. As for us, we think that the mind becomes evil through dwelling on fleshly thoughts, but that there is nothing bad in the body, since the body is not evil in itself.[98]

The perpetual remembrance of God which the Hesychasts practice, is a consciously willed action which also involves the body. In the same way as waking, fasting and prostrations are called ascetic exercises, so also inner prayer is an ascetic practice which requires bodily discipline. *"For this body which is united to us,"* Gregory says, *"has been attached to us as a fellow-worker by God, or rather placed under our control. Thus we will repress it, if it is in revolt, and accept it, if it conducts itself as it should."*[99]

Gregory insists that the body has a God-given ability both to receive and to integrate spiritual qualities:

(...) the spiritual joy which comes from the mind into the body is in no way corrupted by the communion with the body, but transforms the body and makes it spiritual, because it then rejects all the evil appetites of the body; it no longer drags the soul downwards, but is elevated together with it. (...) What of Stephen, the first martyr, whose face, even while he was yet living, shone like the face of an angel? Did not his body also experience divine things?[100]

The Uncreated Light

What indeed is the light which radiates from Christ at Tabor? What does it say to us of God? What effects does it have on man? For Gregory the light of Tabor is God's uncreated energy, while for Barlaam it is a created reality which functions as a divine symbol. According the Gregory it is just as misleading to call the light of Tabor a symbol as to call the eucharist a symbol.

98. Gregory Palamas, ibid., I.ii.1, p. 41.
99. Ibid., II.ii.5, p. 48.
100. Ibid., II.ii.9, p. 51.

For the eucharist *is* God through the power of consecration, and the light of Tabor *is* God in being God's energy. And the energy of God is just as much God as the essence of God. The difference is that God's essence is transcendent and therefore unattainable, while God's energy is immanent and therefore attainable. We recognize this argumentation from the period of iconoclasm. Then as well, the battle raged over the relationship between the material and the divine. In order to defend icons John of Damascus referred to the Incarnation, and in order to defend Hesychasm Gregory Palamas referred to the Transfiguration. The uncreated light

> transforms the body, and communicates its own splendour to it when, miraculously, the light which deifies the body becomes accessible to the bodily eyes. Thus indeed did the great Arsenius appear when engaged in hesychastic combat; similarly Stephen, whilst being stoned, and Moses, when he descended from the mountain.[101]

Gregory explains here what happens when the body of a saint becomes visibly shining. The transfigured man is not only illuminated, but also *made translucent* by the uncreated light such that the body, according to Symeon the New Theologian's own experience, becomes *"transformed into light."* Therewith can *"the face of Abba Pambo shine like lightning"* and Abba Arsenius look *"as if he were a flame."* *"God is light,"* the Scripture says I John 1:5. The holy ones who live in mystical union with God become themselves light. Gregory says of Paul that he *"was light and spirit, to which he was united. (. . .)"* *"However,"* he adds, *"in attaining this condition, the divine Paul could not participate absolutely in the divine essence. (. . .)"*[102]

---

101. Ibid., II.iii.9, p. 57.

102. Ibid., II.iii.37, p. 66: Because of the accusation that Hesychasm is a form of Messalianism, Gregory wishes to emphasize that the divine light which the mystic experiences is not the transcendent nature or essence of God, but the immanent glory or energy of God. Gregory also rejects the claim that he has introduced a duality in the nature of God by differentiating between the essence and the energies of God: "For one applies the word 'sun' to the rays as well as to the source of the rays; yet it does not follow that there are two suns. There is, then, a single God, even though one says that the deifying grace is *from* God. The light is also one of the things that 'surround' the sun, yet it is certainly not the essence of the sun. So how could the light which shines from God upon the saints be the essence of God?" (III.iii.11, p. 108).

Since the uncreated light is *immaterial,* it is not necessarily available to sensory perception. In order to comprehend this light, the natural senses must be cleansed by grace. *"This spiritual light is thus not only the object of the vision,"* Gregory explains further, *"but it is also the power by which we see; it is neither a sensation nor an intellection, but is a spiritual power. (...)"*[103] It is therefore said of the witness who saw Abba Arsenios illuminated by uncreated fire that *"the brother was worthy to look upon such things."* His senses had already been cleansed.

Gregory emphasizes that the created man is not necessarily able to fathom the uncreated energies of God:

> Do you not see that these divine energies are in God, and remain invisible to the created faculties? Yet the saints see them, because they have transcended themselves with the help of the Spirit.[104]

When Abba Joseph says to Abba Lot: *"If thou wilt, thou shalt be made wholly a flame,"* this is a radical appeal to transcend oneself in order to seek mystical union with God. Again it is a question of a reciprocal influence between human will and divine grace. As God transcends himself in order to take part in human nature, so man transcends himself in order to partake of divine nature. The motivating factor behind these processes is love. *"We love, because he first loved us"* (I John 4:19), says the apostle John. Gregory presents this dialectic in the following way:

> Every virtue and imitation of God on our part indeed prepares those who practise them for divine union, but the mysterious union itself is effected by grace.[105]

Another quality of the uncreated light is that it is infinite, *"as a limitless sea."*[106] The uncreated light has always been and will always be. When Christ according to the liturgical texts reveals *"an indistinct ray of his divin-*

---

103. Ibid., III.ii.14, p. 100.
104. Ibid., III.iii.10, p. 107.
105. Ibid., III.i.27, p. 83.
106. Ibid., III.i.33, p. 88.

ity" which usually is *"hidden by the flesh,"*[107] we understand that the light the disciples saw at Tabor is a quality both of the preexistent, the incarnate, the glorified and the Christ who is to come again (parousia).

Since the light which transforms the saints into a greater likeness of God is according to its nature eternal, so also spiritual growth continues eternally. Because the uncreated light is limitless, it will always be possible to see and to receive more. Here Gregory Palamas develops further the idea of perpetual progress or deification. This thought is explicitly expressed in *The Life of Moses* by Gregory of Nyssa and *The Ladder of Divine Ascent* by John Climacus.

In reference to the calling of the divine name "light," Dionysius the Areopagite explains that God "bestows at first a tempered radiance; then when they taste the light as it were and *desire more,* he gives it in greater measure and shines upon them more abundantly because they have loved much, and ever uplifts them to things beyond, according to their power of gazing upward."[108] In other words God takes into account that man is finite and created, and adjusts the measure of light in relation to the capacity of the receiver. He makes himself dependent upon the receiver "desiring more."

Translucent Man

In 1378 Theophane the Greek decorated a church in Novgorod which was called "The Tranfiguration of our Saviour in the Elias-street." The monumental frescoes are still unusually expressive, in spite of the damage incurred by overpainting, restoration and fire. The colour scale is greatly reduced, the facial features and drapery are almost completely erased in many places. These changes, however, do not reduce the content or the power of the work's expression. The changes entail of course a loss, but can also be interpreted positively, such as we see the wear and tear which has value in its own right. Among these fresco fragments we find a representation of the holy Macarios of Egypt. He is a representation of how man's "theosis" involves both body, soul and spirit (plate 13).

107. Ibid., III.i.12, p. 15 and 15, p. 76.
108. Dionysius the Areopagite, *Divine Names,* IV, p. 34.

The saint is frontally depicted. He lifts up his hands as in prayer. The body language reflects a listening and open attitude. There are no precise transitions between the hair, the beard and the clothing. These elements are blended together creating an even greyish white background for the terracotta skin colour of the hands, feet and face. Only a weak contour separates the figure from the background colour which is also greyish white, and the halo repeats the skin colour. Theophane paints the bright white highlights with just a few well-placed brushstrokes. Such as the fresco appears today, there are no nuances between carnation and highlights. The resulting effect can be called expressive minimalism. The simple colour harmonies which do not correspond to the original colours work together to make the intense impression that we stand in front of a mystic who has allowed himself to be totally absorbed by the divine presence.[109] The minimalistic pictorial language emphasizes central contemplative values such as simplicity, humility and spiritual eagerness. Form and content are one.

This painting is not primarily a physical portrait, even though the outer features such as the long hair and beard, the garments made of skin and a body which bears signs of extented asceticism correspond with the historical facts. Macarios appears in an ecstatic, deified state, completely permeated and transformed by the uncreated light. He resembles that which he contemplates. He both sees light and is light.

Macarios radiates the glory Adam had before the fall, a glory which was won back in and through the Incarnation and Transfiguration. The liturgical texts solemnly proclaim what the Transfiguration of Christ means anthropologically when it states that *"Transfigured, thou hast made Adam's nature, which was grown dim, to shine once more as lightning, transforming it into the glory and splendour of thy Godhead."* It is further stated that the Transfigura-

---

109. The Russian art historian Lazarev interprets the extremely contrasting colours in Theophane the Greek's painting as an iconographical argument against Hesychasm. He claims that the contrast between local colours and the highlights is an expression for the distance between the human and the divine and attributes to Theophane a dualistic world view. Since one cannot necessarily deduce ideology from form, such an interpretation seems highly unlikely. In the present study both Theophane the Greek's Transfiguration icon and the actual fresco of Macarios are, if not directly, then indirectly, seen as appropriate to the spirituality which Hesychasm represents. At this time Hesychasm had the status of official doctrine. See the discussion of this subject in Jostein Børtnes, *Visions of Glory,* pp. 105-109.

tion reveals *"the original beauty of the image."*[110] It is this "original beauty" Theophane the Greek shows in his depiction of the transfigured Macarios. According to the mystic's own words this state can be characterized as:

> The soul becomes the "throne of God," it becomes altogether light, altogether a face, altogether an eye; each of its members filled with light, no place is left for darkness, as if it were full of spiritual eyes; on all sides it is a "face" turned toward God, receiving the light of Christ which enters within.[111]

Translucent Matter

In the formal analysis of Theophane the Greek's Transfiguration icon we discussed how the combination of gold leaf and transparent egg tempera colour creates the impression that light penetrates matter and in this way makes the entire landscape shine from within. Because the Transfiguration of Christ is understood as a prefiguration of the resurrection and the glory of the coming world, not only man, but also the rest of creation is included in the event. We shall therefore continue to let this icon be the basis of our study of the *cosmological* aspects of the Transfiguration.

It is in particular the way the *light* appears in the picture which indicates that this is a supernatural event. The technical challenge in painting is to depict how the uncreated light influences its surroundings as opposed to sunlight or any other light source. It is for this reason that the two groups which show Jesus and the disciples on the way up to and down from the mountain are enveloped in darker tones. In the same way the two groups of angels who collect Moses and Elijah from their heavenly abode are wrapped in blue grey colour tones. This is most likely done in order to show that the life the prophets now live transcends the life the disciples know. The colours also emphasize the uniqueness of the Tabor light.

110. Liturgical excerpts from the feast of the Transfiguration, celebrated the sixth of August. Quoted after Kallistos Ware, "The Transfiguration of the Body," *Sacrament and Image*, p. 29.

111. Macarios of Egypt, "Homily 1, 2," quoted after Vladimir Lossky, *Vision of God*, p. 114.

The formal analysis has revealed that the highlights which accentuate the face, clothing and mountain tops originate from different angles outside of the pictorial plane. The uncreated light does not limit itself or let itself be modified by the categories of this life. The so-called "sent light," represented by the gilded background and the transparent colours, looks as though it comes in from a source behind the icon itself. This effect can be interpreted as the Prime Mover's absolute presence in the form of light.[112] Symeon the New Theologian explains that the uncreated light is "radiant as the sun and (. . .) that it *encompasses the whole of creation.*"[113]

The three blue rays of light which beam from the mandorla behind the transfigured Christ come from a light source which is clearly *darker* than the rays nearest Christ. The *"Darkness is as the light"* (Ps. 139:12), says David. We glimpse here "the divine darkness" which Dionysius the Areopagite defined thus: *"The divine darkness is the unapproachable light where it is said God lives."*[114] God the Father's transcendence is revealed as darkness, while the immanence of the Son shows itself as light.

The Hesychast and monastic founder Gregory of Sinai (ca. 1265–1346) sees the Tabor light as a manifestation of the Trinity:

And as the Son shone ineffably on Tabor in the light of his power, they clearly discerned the Father of lights through that voice from above and the Spirit through the resplendent cloud, and recognised the Trinity as an everlasting outpouring of light and brightness, truly flashing forth like lightning in the transfigured Christ.

Gregory goes on to expound upon the cosmological aspects of the Transfiguration:

Then even the mountains rejoiced and were glad — as is said, "Tabor and Hermon rejoice in Thy name" — and heaven exulted and all the earth leapt with joy, seeing on the mountain their own master shin-

112. This is not Polyteism, but an expression of God being by his energies continually present in all of creation.

113. Symeon the New Theologian, *The Discourses,* p. 201.

114. Dionysios the Areopagite, "Letter 5," quoted after Kallistos Ware, "Studies of Spirituality," p. 253.

ing more brightly than the sun both sensibly and intelligibly, and illuminating and sanctifying all things. (. . .) The powers, looking down from above, shuddered; and the earth, from below, trembled with joy and fear. Thus all creation, all nature, "every thing that hath breath" praised, glorified and magnified Him, seeing its master and king, who had shown through previously as founder, as creator, now transfigured and transformed on the mountain and resplendent beyond the sun as God. (. . .)[115]

As was mentioned earlier, the Transfiguration of Jesus points towards his resurrection and ascension. After the resurrection the glorified body of Jesus can pass through closed doors (John 20:19, 26). His body appears to have superseded the natural laws to which other bodies are subject. When the disciples doubt that this is a real body, but rather a spirit, Jesus says: *"handle me, and see; for a spirit has not flesh and bones as you see that I have"* (Luke 24:39). It is a fully real, but nevertheless completely different body which *"ascended up to heaven and took its seat at the right hand of the Father."*[116] In Christ the nature of man has taken its seat at the throne of heaven.

The Gospels tell that the Master healed sickness, raised the dead, turned water into wine and caused the storm to subside. These miracles are not only a demonstration of the power of God (energeia), but also a sign of creation's ability to recognize and obey the Creator. If we omit attributing to created matter this ability to in some way "conciously respond," matter will be understood as dead and therefore just a thing.[117] When the Scriptures therefore say that *"then shall all the trees of the wood sing for joy"* (Ps. 96:12) and *"let the floods clap their hands; let the hills sing for joy together"*

---

115. Gregory the Sinaiite, *Discourse on the Transfiguration*, §24, p. 49.

116. Paraphrased from the Nicene Creed.

117. In the article "Body and Matter in Spiritual Life" from the collection of articles *Sacrament and Image* Anthony Bloom explains the laws of nature which apply after the Fall as "iron rules." He reasons that all of creation has a consciousness of God which became inhibited through the Fall, but which nevertheless is capable to comprehend glimpses of the Creator's presence. He claims that if we understand matter as dead, opaque and heavy, the supernatural works of Jesus are no longer miracles, but magic, manipulative acts wrought upon a passive nature.

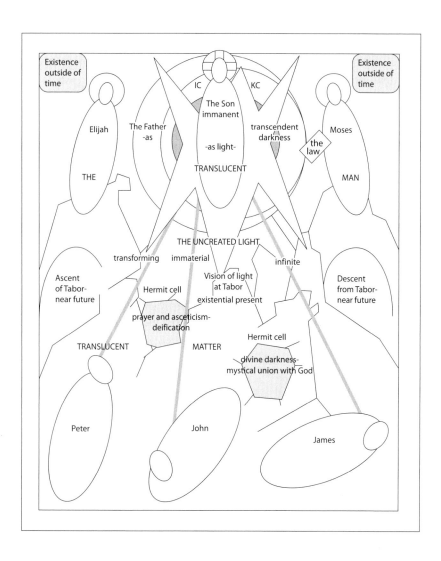

(Ps. 98:8), this is more than a beautiful, poetic expression. In addition to reflecting a basic connection between the material and the divine, such expressions disclose that the entire cosmos will some day partake in the fruit of the incarnation.

Both among the Desert Fathers and in later literature of the saints there are instances where wild animals live in peaceful fellowship with sanctified ascetics. It seems as though the animals sense that these people represent powers of a new and better existence.

> In the same place of Sapsas, there dwelt in a cave another old man of so great virtue that he would welcome the lions into his cave with him, and offer them food in his lap: so full of divine grace was the man of God.[118]

On the basis of the interpretation we have given of the Transfiguration icon, we can establish the model on page 110.

118. John Mochus, "Pratum Spirituale" in Helen Waddell, *The Desert Fathers,* p. 250. See also pp. 254-257.

Chapter III

THE DESCENT

Concluding Summary, on the Basis of the Analysis and Interpretation of the Transfiguration

From Vision to Reflection

A certain mental adjustment is needed in order to descend from Tabor. Distance from that which we have witnessed there can make it easier to see the connection between the different aspects of the Transfiguration. In this third and final phase we shall reflect on what we have in fact discussed in the two preceding phases. A review would help us to know what conclusions this study can allow us to draw.

"The Ascent" entails a presentation and analysis of limited iconographical material. "The Vision of Light" applies a selection of textual sources pertaining to this material. To choose involves evaluation. A certain foreknowledge is required in order to select iconographical material and relevant theological literature. This selection is made in light of the fact that a comparative analysis is interesting only if we can confirm differences in the material we are to compare. In order to obtain a limited, yet varied selection, it was necessary to include widely diverging versions of the Transfiguration motif. The datings represent a time span of about 900 years.

The time span is even greater when we consider the theological literature. If we include the New Testament texts, the distance between the oldest and the most recent texts is about 1,300 years.

Earlier we commented on the close interaction between iconography and theology in the Eastern church. It remains, however, to find an answer to how we should understand the relationship between iconographical and theological development. Do these changes occur in parallel? Do the texts give a basis for new ways of presenting the motif or was the motif read and interpreted differently in accordance with new theological problems and issues? Is it the motif or the interpretation of it which changes?

Iconographical Variation and Theological Precision

As we commence our descent from Tabor, we shall first say a few words about the chosen iconographical material which provides the basis for this study. The two preiconoclastic representations of the Transfiguration, namely the apse mosaics in the Monastery of Saint Catherine and Sant Apollinare in Classe, are the only monumental mosaics from this period which present this motif in an almost unaltered state. If we keep in mind that these works comprise the main decoration in two contemporaneous basilicas, built during the reign of the emperor who also built Hagia Sophia in Constantinople, we can rightly say that we are dealing with artwork of unique quality and value.

As mentioned earlier, the Sinai mosaic gives a figurative representation of the Transfiguration, while the Ravenna mosaic is mainly symbolic. These highly differentiated solutions of the same motif make for a rather interesting comparison. Such marked variations are not found in later post-iconoclastic schemes.

Of the remaining versions it is the Ottonian manuscript illumination which seems to stand out from the rest. But since this version cannot be defined as Byzantine, we are not able to include it in the Byzantine comparative material. Both the mosaic in Sant Apollinare in Classe and the Ottonian manuscript illumination represent exceptions to the other Transfiguration motifs. The Eastern, Byzantine Ravenna mosaic can be associated with the Western cultural sphere through its geographic location, while the Western, Ottonian manuscript illumination can be associated with the Eastern sphere of culture through its Byzantine prototype. Both have Latin inscriptions. In Ravenna Greek and Latin were used as liturgical languages. In the German kingdom, also called the Holy Roman Empire, Latin was the natural liturgical language.

Between the Byzantine apse mosaic in Sinai and the Russian icon attributed to Theophane the Greek, there is a span of about 850 years. Because of the great distance in time, together with the widely varying technique and format, their great similarity in form is quite remarkable. Peter and John have changed places. Otherwise the placement of the figures is the same. The difference is that the mosaic lacks a landscape which would create a sense of space, while the landscape is an important part of the icon. The Transfiguration scene itself in the Sinai mosaic stands out from the other versions precisely through the economization of effects. The only elements in addition to the six persons are an almond-shaped mandorla, eight rays of light and three stripes of colour indicating the ground.

If we evaluate all of the chosen pictorial material, and ignore the mosaic from Ravenna and the Ottonian manuscript illumination, it would be more appropriate to call the changes *variations* on a theme than a development in a particular direction. The word "development" is problematic because it so easily leads our mind into a normative train of thought. We therefore limit ourselves to confirming that there are variations, but that these variations occur within a relatively consistent iconographical tradition.

This remarkable degree of consistency can be attributed to the canonical status of Orthodox iconography. The artisan is subordinate to dogmatic discipline. The dogmas function as protective and regulative premises for the character of faith and its presentation. Without such a frame of reference both the content and expression of faith are in danger of relativization. As we have mentioned earlier, dogmas cannot be exhaustive statements of divine truths. The same can be said about the visual representation of faith. Neither words not images made by man can depict a divine mystery adequately. This acknowledgement is expressed through the apophatic theology of the Eastern church.

We have called changes in the motif *variations* on a theme. Accordingly, we can say that changes in the understanding of the motif represent a further deepening and a greater precision of the theological content. In other words, we have a much richer tradition of interpretation within which to view the motif in the fifteenth century than we have in the sixth century. Even though the central dogmatic teaching on the Trinity and the two natures of Christ was formulated already at the councils of Nicea (325) and Chalcedon (451), there was still a need for greater precision concerning the nature of God, the nature of man, the physical universe and their interrelationship. Iconoclasm of the eighth and ninth centuries and Hesychasm in the fourteenth century were among factors which predicated the need for this further precision.

As we know, "The Triumph of Orthodoxy" in 847 established that the icon was deemed dogmatically authoritative. John of Damascus and Theodore the Studite reasoned that the gradual self-revelation of God, which reached a climax when God descended into matter, had to affect the view of what function visual representations should have in the Church. "The Triumph of Hesychasm" in 1341 entailed a radical yet logical development of what spiritual effects this fundamental theological thought could have. By insisting that man only relates truly to God as an integrated entity of body, soul and spirit, the Hesychasts managed to emphasize that deification encompasses the whole man. Neither "The Triumph of Orthodoxy" nor "The Triumph of Hesychasm" represented in themselves anything qualitatively new in relation to the theological tradition. Briefly, we can say that the iconodules reflected over the mystery of the Incarnation, while the Hesychasts dwelt upon the mystery of the Transfiguration. Common to both these "triumphs" is the conciliar decision that matter can both receive, contain and communicate that which is genuinely spiritual. The question then is, whether or not this theological deepening and precision can be deduced from the iconography.

We maintain that the changes which in the course of time occurred in the *representation* of the motif can not necessarily be attributed to changes in the *understanding* of the motif. Holding in mind the principle that theology comes before iconography, it could be that changes in theology resulted in changes in iconography. The selected material in this study, although not systematically chosen, gives a representative selection, yet is not a substantial basis for drawing such conclusions. The theology becomes richer and the motif more varied, but as it has been shown from our interpretation, it is more natural to read theology *into* the motif than *from* it.

When we interpret the icon of Theophane the Greek in the light of Hesychasm, it is not because this type of spirituality can be directly deduced from any specific iconographical features. To see mountain grottos in the landscape as hermit cells and the dark blue colour tone in the mandorla as divine darkness is a possible, but not a necessary interpretation. Likewise, the transparent effect from the egg tempera technique is a means of creating the impression that the landscape is lit from within. The form emphasizes the content. The lack of landscape in the Sinai mosaic does not mean that the idea of a transfigured cosmos was not sufficiently developed at the time the mosaic was designed. To place importance on the landscape in the contemporary Ravenna mosaic indicates something else.

It is hardly possible to reconstruct the situation within which the sixth-century viewer interpreted these art works, but knowledge of the prevailing theological issues of the time makes it easier to sketch a plausible frame of reference. The condemnation of various heretical christologies of that time gives us reason to assume that the dogmatic aspect of images was emphasized both by the theologically responsible designer and by the theologically educated viewer. Here we deduce meaning *from theology to iconography*. We can also deduce such *from iconography to theology* by using the gold background, the rays of light and the ecstatic facial expressions of the disciples as a reference point for interpreting the mosaic as a correlative to the Orthodox mysticism of light. We see that theology and iconography refer to each other. The art work is not autonomous, but related to a context and therefore open to various interpretations. By focusing on different contextual aspects such as we have done in the interpretive part of this study, different aspects of the art works emerge and become relevant for the viewer.

This general observation naturally pertains also to the other versions of the Transfiguration motif. Individual works remain unchanged, in so far as they have not been changed by damage, by restoration, etc. Yet, as a bearer of many meanings, the art work can express different facets of these meanings all according to who is viewing it and within which context it is being viewed.

A viewer who looks at the Sinai mosaic today, and who is familiar with the relevant interpretative tradition, has a larger frame of reference, and therefore also an eye which sees more than another viewer who saw the same mosaic during the sixth century. Seeing and understanding is guided by what the viewer has seen and already knows. The interpretation of the art work varies according to the viewer's competence. In other words, it is not the art work which changes, but the perception of it.

Sinai and Ravenna

If we juxtapose reproductions of the two monumental Byzantine mosaics from Sinai and Ravenna, we see that the differences are more apparent than the likenesses. Both are identified as representations of the Transfiguration, but because the decoration in Sant Apollinare in Classe combines the different motifs by means of symbolism, the interpretation of it is more complicated. In particular, the cross medallion mediates several layers of meaning. To give such a prominent place to a person who historically cannot be connected to the Transfiguration strengthens the impression that it is not the depiction of a biblical event which is the main intention here. Rather, it is an adaption of the event. The conspicuous placement which the transfigured Christ has in the Sinai mosaic is given to Bishop Apollinaris in the Ravenna mosaic. Apollinaris is not placed in a mandorla, but as we have shown, the context indicates that the bishop and martyr is represented both in a deified and a glorified state. The mosaic in Sant Apollinare in Classe visualizes the saint's function as example and intercessor for the congregation. In addition, the designers of this decoration have clearly intended to make Ravenna a city of religious authority and political power.

Since the actual basilicas were built under the reign of the same emperor with only sixteen years difference, it is not improbable that those responsible for these apse mosaics could have known of each other. Whether these projects were planned in cooperation is unknown, but the mosaics seem in any case to be intended for different types of viewers.

In Sant Apollinare in Classe the decoration is seen by clerics and laymen who take part in the liturgy of the mass. The relationship between the bishop and his congregation is depicted as that of a shepherd and his flock. Through alternating biblical and liturgical texts the congregation is reminded of the saving works which comprise the promise of hope for that future life they see in the mosaic. Through the sacrament of the eucharist the officiating priest or bishop shares a fortaste of the perfect life in the world to come.

In the monastery of Saint Catherine, the decoration is seen by monks whose life is dedicated to asceticism and prayer. The mosaic invites the monks to a spiritual ascent by following Moses up to Sinai and the disciples of Jesus up to Tabor. The congregation of Sant Apollinare in Classe is witness to an *eschatological* vision, while the monks of Saint Catherine are witness to a *mystical* vision.

In the Sinai mosaic, the disciples are characterized both by ecstatic tension and by elevated calm. Even though they are shown in an extraordinary and awesome situation, their gestures are nevertheless relatively controlled. The transfigured Christ appears in divine majesty and power. This is not the vulnerable Son of Man who is placed under human conditions, but the triumphant and unconquerable Son of God. For, as Gregory Palamas points out: *"The saviour did not ascend Tabor, accompanied by the chosen disciples, in order to show them that he was a man. (. . .) No, he went up to show them that he was the radiance of the Father."*[1]

In the Ravenna mosaic, the disciples are represented as sheep without individual characteristics. The transfigured Christ is shown as a face inscribed in a cross. Those participating are represented as signs, not as actual persons. The exception is Moses and Elijah who are presented in half figure, and in this way take on a certain sense of reality. Only Apollinaris is depicted as a fully recognizable person. This type of abstraction leads the viewer to passive reflection more than to emotional involvement.

The Sinai mosaic expresses *the personal* spiritual experience by representing historical persons in direct relationship with the self-revealed energies of God. The Ravenna mosaic shows *the collective* spiritual experience by focusing on the service of the flock. The idealized sheep, which symbolize the disciples at Tabor and the fellowship of the congregation, exist in a landscape akin to paradise where the divine presence is shown indirectly by a medallion cross and a saint. There is an essential difference between *a factual divine presence* exemplified by uncreated fire or light, and *a sign of divine presence* exemplified by the Christ-symbol or a sanctified person.

1. Gregory Palamas, *The Triads,* III.i.19, p. 78.

Moses and Apollinaris

Historically Moses is associated with Sinai and Apollinaris with Ravenna. The correlation between the placement of a church and a local saint is expressed by both mosaics. The visionary leader, giver of the law and mystic, Moses, spoke with God "face to face" (Exod. 33:11). Bishop Apollinaris was mystically joined with the sacrifice of Christ through his martyrdom. Moses functions as a model for the monk or abbot while Apollinaris is a model for the officiating priest or bishop.

The radical monastic life can be seen as an alternative to martyrdom. The monk resembles the martyr by a definitive separation from the world and an unconditional commitment to God. After forsaking the secular life for the contemplative life, the monk is no longer his own master. In the ascetic literature of the time it is often repeated how decisively important it is for the monk to have an adviser, a so-called "spiritual father," towards whom he can be obedient, tell his thoughts to and from whom he can receive guidance. A spiritual father is responsible to God for the monk under his care. John Climacus presents Moses as the prototype for such a spiritual father:

> Those of us who wish to get away from Egypt, to escape from Pharaoh, need some Moses to be our intermediary with God, to stand between action and contemplation.[2]

Here John gives an allegorical interpretation of an example where Moses intercedes for the children of Israel under attack from the hostile Amalekites (Exod. 17:11-13). When Moses tires, his hands are held up by Hur, who represents action, and Aaron, who represents contemplation. The monk needs help in order to find the right balance between action (praxis), which pertains to the ascetic battle to overcome vices and to develop virtues, and contemplation (theoria), which pertains to the mystical vision of God with the inner eye. In this way the Israelites triumph over the Amalekites, in other words, the passions, with the help of intercession from Moses, the spiritual leader.[3]

---

2. John Climacus, *The Ladder of Divine Ascent,* Step 1, On Renunciation of Life, p. 75.

3. This interpretation is from a footnote in *The Ladder of Divine Ascent,* p. 75.

Apollinaris resembles Moses in that he has a representative function before God. The congregation has in this holy bishop both an example and an intercessor.

Abbot and Bishop

In the Ravenna mosaic the hierarchical structure of the Church is greatly accentuated by five bishops in full liturgical garb. In the Sinai mosaic there are two clerics who probably were connected with the monastery during its construction, namely the deacon John and the abbot Longinus. These received a less conspicuous but no less honorary place in the circle of prophets and apostles who frame the Transfiguration scene. Such an incorporation of local leaders in a biblical portait gallery reflects the wish to establish a continuity between the Old and the New Testaments and the tradition of the Church. In this way both mosaics express a form of ecclesiastical self-insight.

At this point we will also look closely at that which characterizes a monastic church as opposed to the bishop's seat. This is not a nuanced historical analysis of how the situation actually was in Sinai and Ravenna during the sixth and seventh centuries, but some general reflections over the characteristics of churches built in such different locations as a desert and a harbor city.

The bishop and the abbot have different natures as persons of authority. The bishop is usually stationed in the city, he controls large economic resources and has many administrative responsibilities. It is difficult for him to be personally acquainted with everyone for whom he has formal responsibility. Together with his colleagues, the bishop regulates the Church's relationship to political powers, formulates dogma and protects true doctrine. A potential danger for a leader in such a position is corruption based upon power and privilege.

The abbot resides in a monastery and lives in close fellowship with those monks for whom he is responsible. He is chosen by the monks on the basis of his personal qualities as a spiritual authority. The ideal abbot has his mandate not only because of his office but because of a holy life. The abbot is responsible for fellowship faithfully following the liturgical rhythm of the monastery. He is called to convey contemplative experience and to develop spiritual growth in the monks through his own example. An obvious temptation for a monastic leader is spiritual pride.

Stated simply, we can say that the bishop represents the official, hierarchically structured ecclesiastial authority, while the abbot represents the spiritual ecclesiastical authority founded on his own person. Despite the distance between the bishop's residence and the cell of the abbot, it would be misguided to see these offices as opposites. Bishops were often recruited from a monastic milieu,[4] and we find examples of the spiritual, wise man seeking shelter in the wilderness on account of deeper needs in himself and others.[5] The bishop and the abbot represent different areas of responsibility in the Church which cannot be seen in isolation. On the contrary they are dependent upon each other and work to correct each other.

Bishop Maximian, who was bishop of Ravenna between 546 and 556, can serve as a prototype for a bishop responsible for the areas referred to above. Likewise we can mention John Climacus as an example of a personally integrated spiritual leader. Against his own will he was called out of his hermit cell in order to be abbot of the monastery of Saint Catherine. The spiritual maxims recorded in the book *The Ladder of Divine Ascent* were originally written for the monks at Saint Catherine. This book is still read aloud in Orthodox monasteries during Lent.

From the Formal to the Ecstatic

Those aspects we have especially considered in the interpretation of the Sinai mosaic are — from the top to the bottom — *the mystical, the liturgical and the dogmatic.* With a similar reading of the Ravenna mosaic we can em-

---

4. The monastic founder, liturgical author and bishop Basil the Great (of Caesarea) appointed his younger brother Gregory, who preferred to live a quiet, monastic life, to be bishop of Nyssa. Basil did this because of a pressing need to emphasize Orthodox christology among the bishops where the majority were Arian.

5. In the biography of Anthony the Great it is told how he, after having been discovered as a holy ascetic and wise man, withdraws himself to the desert in order to concentrate on spiritual matters. After a period as abbot of the monastery of Saint Catherine, John Climacus returns to his hermit cell outside the monastery where he lives out his original calling.

phasize *the eschatological, the sacramental and the hierarchical.* All these aspects are implicitly present in both mosaics, but in different ways and to different degrees.

In the representation of the post-iconoclastic Transfiguration motif — here exemplified by Theophane the Greek's version — we observe an accentuation of the psychological reactions of the disciples. The distance between the transfigured Christ and the disciples increases and the emotional effect of what they see becomes more emphasized. This growing interest in the *anthropological* aspect seems to apply to the latter half of the fourteenth century. Is there perhaps a connection between the change in iconographical accent and the change in theological accent?

Based upon what we know of the Hesychastic struggle and its final outcome, it is not unreasonable to think that there may be such a connection. Without determining what is the cause and what is the effect, we notice a correlation in time between "the triumph of Hesychasm" and the establishing of this iconographical convention. Several prominent iconographers received spiritual impulses, artistic training and commissions within the monastic environment where the Hesychastic spirituality developed.

Gregory the Sinaiite discloses that he is familiar with dramatic, visual depictions of the Transfiguration when he describes the disciples' reactions thus:

> And astonished in mind and overcome by the divine light, *they fell to the earth, one on his back, the other face downward,* oppressed by the brightness which welled out from the fount of light; and as though encompassed, they were frozen to the spot. But *Peter woke up* and perceived his glory, amazed at the frightening nature of the unexpected sight; and in his consternation, seeing the two men, Moses and Elijah, standing together at his side, he said to Jesus, "Master, it is good for us to be here" and then "Let us make three tabernacles, one for each," not knowing what he was saying, his mind being *in a state of entrancement and inebriation.*[6]

A Russian festival icon of the late fifteenth century, painted in the style of the Novgorod school, corresponds well to this detailed description (plate

6. Gregory the Sinaiite, *Discourse on the Transfiguration,* 6 12, p. 31.

15). Here we see how the disciples *"fell to the earth, one on his back (James), the other face downward (John), oppressed by the brightness which welled out from the fount of light."* The three rays of light which spring from the mandorla seem to hit the disciples with great force. Likewise we notice that "Peter woke up and perceived his glory." Gregory of Sinai comments on the suggestion of Peter to build three huts as an expression of confusion — *"his mind being in a state of entrancement and inebriation."*

Another Russian festival icon painted by Andrei Rublev in 1405 (plate 14), has many similarities to the version we have just referred to. The placement of the figures is the same and their gestures are similar, but we also discern differences.

In the Novgorod icon the disciples are struck by a beam of light which throws them to the ground. Through varied use of colour, animated gesticulation and fluttering drapery, the icon painter clearly shows the outer drama of the transfiguration.

In Andrei Rublev's icon the light is not shown as individual beams. The disciples are enveloped in a sea of light, and there is something rather lethargic about them. It is uncertain whether James is at all aware that he is falling. We have the impression that he floats or falls onto a soft surface. The knees are slightly bent and his left hand rests in his lap. He holds his right hand over his mouth as a sign of surprise, but the rest of his body seems powerless. He stares with wide-open eyes at the unfathomable — that the Lord is changing appearance — and he is spellbound. John holds his head as if he has just woken from a "deep sleep" (Luke 9:32). Peter kneels with his back to the scene while he cautiously turns his face and looks behind him. He holds both hands out in front of himself as if to regain his balance. Still we see no signs which indicate that he will speak.

If we look again at the Novgorod icon, we see that John falls forward in the same direction as James. While Rublev's icon shows John at the moment when he is waking up from the shock of the experience, here he is caught in the middle of the fall. Yet still there is more reflection than drama in the way he is represented. He holds his right hand over the bridge of his nose such that one eye shows. His gaze seems to be directed inward, scared and distant.

When Symeon the New Theologian tells of his ecstatic vision of light, he also touches upon the physical changes which occurred:

It expelled from me all material denseness and bodily heaviness that made my members to be sluggish and numb. It so invigorated and strengthened my limbs and muscles, which had been faint through great weariness, that it seemed to me as though I was stripping myself of the garment of corruption.[7]

The mystic Symeon has here a foretaste of that which will characterize the body after its resurrection. Since the transfiguration is a prefiguration both of the resurrection and the glory in the world to come, we can presume that the disciples might have experienced something similar.

Andrei Rublev seeks to present matter as translucent and the body as weightless. Through a limited range of colour and reduction of outer effects, he succeeds in directing our attention towards the drama occurring at an inner, invisible level.

Since the monk and icon painter Rublev identified himself with Hesychastic ideals, his works are often seen as an expression of Orthodox light-mysticism. Both Rublev's own spiritual orientation and the uniqueness of his work allow for such an interpretation. We note that Moses and Elijah are drawn into the mandorla which surrounds the transfigured Christ. The landscape is bathed in an even, diffused light. The only elements which break the monotony in this landscape are four green bushes and a little mountain cave. The men, the mountain and plants are enveloped in the uncreated and transforming energy which caused Christ to irradiate his divine nature.

Compared to Theophane the Greek's Transfiguration icon (plate 10), which was painted just two years earlier, Andrei Rublev has been very careful with his means. The reason that this icon still makes such a strong impact is perhaps precisely because of the unstated — or the unpainted; the viewer himself must envisage the effect that such a direct experience of the uncreated divine energy has upon created man.[8]

---

7. Symeon the New Theologian, *The Discourses*, p. 201.

8. This observation is an example of how decisive the viewer's attitude is in his meeting with a painting in order for the painting to "communicate itself."

Historical Event and Existential Experience

In ascetic literature we often encounter appeals to learn from that which happened at Tabor. The author draws out qualities of Moses, Elijah or the disciples which are worth striving for. John Chrysostom mentions that the reason that Moses and Elijah appeared in the glory of Tabor is so that the disciples *"would be as humble as Moses, as zealous as Elijah and as full of charity as both."*[9] To focus on the didactic side of the Transfiguration expresses a basic belief about man's potential to develop spiritually. Thus Maximos Confessor interprets the three huts Peter wanted to build as three stages of development:

> These tabernacles represent three stages of salvation, namely that of *virtue,* that of *spiritual knowledge* and that of *theology.* The first requires fortitude and *self-restraint* in the practice of the virtues: of this the type was Elijah. The second requires right *discernment* in natural contemplation: Moses disclosed this in his own person. The third requires the consummate perfection of *wisdom:* this was revealed by the Lord. They were called tabernacles, or temporary dwellings, because beyond them there are other still more excellent and splendid stages, through which those found worthy will pass in the age to be.[10]

Again we see that deification encompasses the whole man. This recurring motif in Byzantine theology reflects an understanding of salvation as a dynamic process where man is made responsible for the degree to which he wishes to regain likeness with God. Maximos Confessor compares the heart of man with the laws of Moses which God wrote with his own finger:

> He who has made his heart pure [I John 3:3] (. . .), *he will in some measure see God himself.* (. . .) When God comes to dwell in such a heart, he honours it by engraving his own letters on it by the Holy Spirit, just as

9. John Chrysostom, *Homilies on the Gospel of Saint Matthew,* Homily 56, The Nicene and Post-Nicene Fathers, Volume X, p. 346.

10. Maximos Confessor, *Two Hundred Texts on Theology and the Incarnate Dispensation of the Son of God,* Second Century, §16, *The Philokalia,* Volume II, p. 141.

he did on the Mosaic tablets [Exod. 31:18]. This he does according to the degree to which the heart, through practice of the virtues and contemplation, has devoted itself to the admonition which bids us, in a mystical sense, "Be fruitful and multiply" [Gen. 35:11]![11]

In addition to this appeal to the will, we find also the call to contemplative, rational and emotional engagement. Gregory of Sinai associates each of the five witnesses to the transfiguration with different virtues which the reader is encouraged to imitate:

> Let us observe with Moses and ascend together with Elijah; let us enquire into divine matters with John and confess our acknowledgement with Peter and approach the light with James, and let us gaze, in so far as possible, on his "glory as of the only begotten from the Father."[12]

Gregory here speaks of how training the sense of spiritual sight in this life represents a preparation for the perfect contemplation of Christ's glory in the life to come. The purpose of these activities is the deification of man — "theosis."

A pervading patristic thought is that man will come to resemble that which he looks at or allows himself to be influenced by. The apostle John, who "enquired into divine matters," says that "we know that when he shall appear, we shall *be like him;* for we shall *see him as he is.*"[13] Based upon such a radical view of what effects visual perception can have on man, it is easier to understand how John of Damascus, after having seen an icon of Christ, can exclaim: *"I have seen God in human form, and my soul has been saved."*[14]

When we claim that we can trace a greater emphasis on the emotional aspect in the iconographical representations of the Transfiguration throughout the fourteenth century, it is not because the call to greater spiri-

---

11. Ibid., 6 80, p. 158.

12. Gregory the Sinaiite, *Discourse on the Transfiguration,* §25, p. 51. Gregory quotes from John 1:14.

13. Ibid., §25, p. 51. Gregory quotes from John 1:14.

14. John of Damascus, *On the Divine Images,* I, 22, p. 30.

tual zeal was anything new. What was new was the need to ascertain that man *can* have direct experience of God, a dogmatic foundation for *why* this is possible together with an explanation of *how* this happens.

The last is the most difficult. For, as Gregory Palamas phrases it, *"Deification is in fact beyond every name. This is why we, who have written much about hesychia (. . .) have never dared hitherto to write about deification."*[15] John Climacus is also reserved in explaining what denoted a mystical experience. Yet ecstatic experiences are a known phenomenon in the monastic milieu he represents, as the following quote witnesses of: *"And in addition to these (quietude and obedience) there is the way of rapture, the way of the mind mysteriously and marvelously carried into the light of Christ."*[16]

Deification can therefore occur both as a gradual process and as a sudden mystical experience. Among other things, Gregory Palamas quotes from liturgical texts in order to substantiate this: *"The chosen apostles were transformed by the divine ecstasy on the mountain, contemplating the irresistable outpouring of your light and your unapproachable Divinity."*[17] In another section he says that *"the transformation of our human nature, its deification and transfiguration — were these not accomplished in Christ from the start, from the moment in which he assumed our nature?"*[18]

One of the burning issues of the Hesychastic conflict is whether that which happened once at Tabor can also be repeated by people other than "the chosen apostles."[19] The question is whether the transfiguration has relevance beyond the purely historical. Gregory Palamas claims that he has the entire patristic tradition behind him when he says that "theosis" is made possible by the incarnation, and that "theosis" in principle and effect is the same as that which Peter, James and John experienced at Tabor. This transformation into greater likeness with God and to which degree it occurs is something man himself has a decisive influence on. Man must make himself available to the uncreated grace.

The descent of God (katabasis) represents a materialization of the di-

15. Gregory Palamas, *The Triads,* III.i.32, p. 87.

16. John Climacus, *The Ladder of Divine Ascent,* Step 26, On Discernment, p. 249.

17. Gregory Palamas, ibid., III.i.23, p. 81.

18. Ibid., III.i.15, p. 76.

19. Here we speak not of the transfiguration of Christ, such as the disciples were witness to, but of man's deification, also called the transfiguration of man.

vine, while the ascent of man (anabasis) represents a deification of the material. A saint reveals the final anthropological consequence of the Incarnation — namely the transfiguration of man. An icon is itself a piece of transfigured matter. It functions both as a reminder of the mystery of the Incarnation and as a celebration of the mystery of the Transfiguration.

The integrated play between word and image in the Orthodox liturgy can be explained as a dynamic *re-presentation* of events in the life of Christ. The liturgy is no static repetition of these experiences, but a sacred act where man allows himself to be made subject to a divine presence. If man is to encounter this presence, he must himself draw near. In the liturgical art of the Byzantine tradition, means such as a gilded background, inverse perspective, frontality and eye contact are consciously used in order to communicate this uncreated, grace-giving presence.

Various representations of the Transfiguration included in this study have this aspect in common. The transfigured Christ transcends the pictorial with his glance. He looks directly at the one who looks at him (plates 2 and 10). Thus the viewer is drawn into an event which occurred *historically*, but which now can occur *existentially* through contemplation and liturgical actualization.

Summary

As mentioned in the introduction, the intention of this study has been to gain greater insight into the connection between the iconographical representation of the Transfiguration and its theological interpretation. During the process of penetrating more deeply into this field of inquiry, an understanding of the Transfiguration as a multifarious expression for the dynamic relationship between theology, anthropology, cosmology — in other words, between God, man and the universe — has crystalized. The Transfiguration motif refers to a supernatural event in the past as well as an indirect visualization of the boldest aspects of the Christian faith, namely the hope of a physical resurrection, a new heaven and a new earth. We have seen that in addition to revealing a glimpse of God's nature, the Transfiguration carries with it a pattern for man's deification (theosis) and a promise of a complete cosmological Transfiguration.

Creation has an intrinsically sacred potential because it is willed by the uncreated God and because the Creator became a creature when he allowed himself to be born as a man. The saving acts of God are tied to factual events in time and space. The sacramental signs which express the uncreated grace of God are physical elements of bread and wine, water and oil. God became physically present and perceivable through the Incarnation and remains physically present and perceivable through the sacraments. When we spoke of the theological legitimization of the icon, we mentioned that the sacramental character of this art can be accounted for by the ability of transformed matter to communicate the sacred. An icon is holy and brings grace because of what it refers to. Yet according to this sacramental view, even the pigments, the gold, the wood, the mosaic tessera, the mortar or parchment on which the holy image is presented will also, in a mystical way, partake in that which is being represented. Thus an icon of the Trans-figuration of Christ takes part in that which it refers to because it intrinsically is a prefiguration of a cosmos penetrated by *the uncreated light*.

APPENDIX

New Testament Texts on the Transfiguration

Matthew 17:1-8

1. And after six days Jesus took with him Peter and James and John his brother, and led them up a high mountain apart. 2. And he was transfigured before them, and his face shone like the sun, and his garments became white as light. 3. And behold, there appeared to them Moses and Elijah, talking with him. 4. And Peter said to Jesus, "Lord, it is well that we are here; if you wish, I will make three booths here, one for you and one for Moses and one for Elijah." 5. He was still speaking, when lo, a bright cloud overshadowed them, and a voice from the cloud said, "This is my beloved Son, with whom I am well pleased; listen to him." 6. When the disciples heard this, they fell on their faces, and were filled with awe. 7. But Jesus came and touched them, saying, "Rise, and have no fear." 8. And when they lifted up their eyes, they saw no one but Jesus only.

Mark 9:2-8

2. And after six days Jesus took with him Peter and James and John and led them up a high mountain apart by themselves; and he was transfigured before them, 3. and his garments became glistening, intensely white, as no fuller on earth could bleach them. 4. And there appeared to them Elijah with Moses; and they were talking to Jesus. 5. And Peter said to Jesus, "Mas-

ter, it is well that we are here; let us make three booths, one for you and one for Moses and one for Elijah." 6. For he did not know what to say, for they were exceedingly afraid. 7. And a cloud overshadowed them, and a voice came out of the cloud, "This is my beloved Son, listen to him." 8. And suddenly looking around they no longer saw anyone with them but Jesus only.

Luke 9:28-36

28. Now about eight days after these sayings he took with him Peter and John and James, and went up on a mountain to pray. 29. And as he was praying, the appearance of his countenance was altered, and his raiment became dazzling white. 30. And behold, two men talked with him, Moses and Elijah, 31. who appeared in glory and spoke of his departure, which he was to accomplish at Jerusalem. 32. Now Peter and those who were with him were heavy with sleep but kept awake, and they saw his glory and the two men who stood with him. 33. And as the men were parting from him, Peter said to Jesus, "Master, it is well that we are here; let us make three booths, one for you and one for Moses and one for Elijah" — not knowing what he said. 34. As he said this, a cloud came and overshadowed them; and they were afraid as they entered the cloud. 35. And a voice came out of the cloud, saying, "This is my Son, my Chosen, listen to him!" 36. And when the voice had spoken, Jesus was found alone.

2 Peter 1:16-18

16. For we did not follow cleverly devised myths when we made known to you the power and coming of our Lord Jesus Christ, but we were eyewitnesses of his majesty. 17. For when he received honor and glory from God the Father and the voice was borne to him by the Majestic Glory, "This is my beloved Son, with whom I am well pleased," 18. we heard this voice borne from heaven, for we were with him on the holy mountain.

Liturgical Texts on the Feast of the Transfiguration[1]

P. 479 Going up with the disciples into the mountain, Thou hast shone forth with the glory of the Father. Moses and Elijah stood at Thy side, for

---

1. *The Festal Menaion.*

the Law and the prophets minister to Thee as God. And the Father, acknowledging Thy natural Sonship, called Thee Son. We praise Him in song together with Thee and the Spirit.

Pp. 479-480 Enlightening the disciples that were with Thee, O Christ our Benefactor, Thou hast shown them upon the holy mountain the hidden and blinding light of Thy nature and of Thy divine beauty beneath the flesh; and they, understanding that Thy glory could not be borne, loudly cried out, "Holy art Thou." For Thou art He whom no man may approach, yet wast Thou seen in the flesh by the world, O Thou who alone lovest mankind.

P. 481 Having uncovered, O Saviour, a little of the light of Thy divinity to those who went up with Thee into the mountain, Thou hast made them lovers of Thy heavenly glory. Therefore they cried in awe: "It is good for us to be here." With them we also sing unto Thee, O Savior Christ who wast transfigured.

P. 489 Thou wast transfigured upon the mountain, and Thy disciples beheld Thy glory, O Christ our God, as far as they were able to do: that when they saw Thee crucified, they might know that Thy suffering was voluntary, and might proclaim unto the world that Thou art truly the brightness of the Father (Heb. 1:3).

P. 476 Transfigured today upon Mount Thabor before the disciples, Christ showed them the nature of man in His own person, arrayed in the original beauty of the Image.

P. 477 Transfigured, Thou hast made the nature that had grown dark in Adam to shine again as lightning, transforming it into the glory and splendour of Thine own divinity.

Liturgical Texts on the Second Sunday in Lent

Memorial of St. Gregory Palamas, Archbishop of Thessalonica[2]

Pp. 315-316 Thy words, inspired by God, are a ladder leading us from earth to heaven, O Gregory, wonder of Thessaly, pray to Christ without ceasing, that we who honour thee may be illuminated with the divine light.

P. 325 All who study thy words and writings, O Gregory, are initiated into the knowledge of God and filled with spiritual wisdom; and they become theologians of the uncreated grace and energy of God.

P. 328 Thou hast become a mirror of God, O Gregory, for thou hast kept without stain that which in thyself is according to the divine image; and bravely establishing thy mind as master over the passions of the flesh, thou hast attained that which is according to God's likeness. So thou hast become the glorious dwelling-place of the Holy Trinity.

P. 329 Hail, glory of the fathers, voice of the theologians, tabernacle of inward stillness, dwelling-place of wisdom, greatest of teachers, deep ocean of the word. Hail, thou who hast practised the virtues of the active life and ascended to the height of contemplation.

Patristic Texts on the Tranfiguration

Origenes of Alexandria (ca. 185–ca. 254)

Commentary on Matthew, The Transfiguration[3]

36. P. 470 The Word has different forms, as He appears to each as is expedient for the beholder, and is manifested to no one beyond the capacity of the beholder.

---

2. *The Lenten Triodion.*
3. "The Ante-Nicene Fathers, Volume X."

38. P. 470 But the garments of Jesus are the expressions and letters of the Gospels with which He invested Himself. But I think that even the words in the Apostles which indicate the truths concerning Him are garments of Jesus, which become white to those who go up into the high mountain along with Jesus. But since there are differences also of things white, His garment become white as the brightest and purest of all white things; and that is light. When therefore you see any one not only with a thorough understanding of the theology concerning Jesus, but also making clear every expression of the Gospels, do not hesitate to say that to Him the garments of Jesus have become white as the light.

39. Pp. 470-471 And perhaps the fullers upon the earth are the wise men of this world who are careful about the diction which they consider to be bright and pure, so that even their base thoughts and false dogmas seem to be beautified by their fulling.

41. P. 472 Peter, as one loving the contemplative life, and having preferred that which was delightsome in it to the life among the crowd with its turmoil, said, with the design of benefiting those who desired it, "It is good for us to be here." But since "love seeketh not its own," Jesus did not do that which Peter thought good; wherefore He descended from the mountain to those who were not able to ascend to it and behold His transfiguration, that they might behold Him in such form as they were able to see Him.

42. Pp. 472-473 Now, I think that God, wishing to dissuade Peter from making three tabernacles, under which so far as it depended on his choice he was going to dwell, shows a tabernacle better, so to speak, and much more excellent, the cloud. For since it is the function of a tabernacle to overshadow him who is in it, and to shelter him, and the bright cloud overshadowed them, God made, as it were, a diviner tabernacle, inasmuch as it was bright, that it might be to them a pattern of the resurrection to come; for a bright cloud overshadows the just, who are at once protected and illuminated and shone upon by it. But what might the bright cloud, which overshadows the just, be? (1) It is, perhaps, the fatherly power, from which comes the voice of the Father bearing testimony to the Son as beloved. (...) (2) And perhaps, too, the Holy Spirit is the bright cloud which overshadows the just, and prophesies of the things of God, who works in it, and says, "This is My beloved Son in whom I am well-pleased"; (3) but I would venture also to say that our Saviour is a bright cloud. (. . .) For a bright cloud of the Father, Son and Holy Spirit overshadows the genuine disciples of Jesus; or a cloud overshadows the Gospl and the law and the prophets, which is bright to him who is able to see the light of it in the Gospel, and the law and the prophets.

43. P. 473 Moses, the law, and Elijah, the prophet, became one only with the Gospel of Jesus; and not, as they were formerly three, did they so abide, but the three became one. (. . .)

Moses and Elijah, having appeared in glory and talked with Jesus, went away to the place from which they had come, perhaps to communicate the words which Jesus spake with them. (. . .)

Wherefore since His being glorified in the resurrection was akin to His transfiguration, and to the vision of His face as the sun, on this account He wishes that these things should then be spoken of by the Apostles, when He rose from the dead.

The Desert Fathers (ca. 250–ca. 400)

On Perpetual Prayer

There came to the abbot Joseph the abbot Lot, and said to him, "Father, according to my strength I keep a modest rule of prayer, fasting, meditation and quiet, and according to my strength I purge my imagination: what more must I do?" The old man, rising, held up his hands against the sky, and his fingers became like ten torches of fire, and he said, "If thou wilt, thou shalt be made wholly a flame."[4]

On Contemplation

A brother went to the cell of abbot Arsenius in Scete, and looked through the window, and saw the old man as it were one flame: now, the brother was worthy to look upon such things. And after he had knocked, the old man

---

4. Quoted after Helen Waddell, *The Desert Fathers,* p. 157.

came out, and saw the brother as one amazed, and said to him, "Hast thou seen aught?" And he answered, "No." And he talked with him, and sent him away.[5]

On the Perfect Life of Some Holy Men

This same abbot Sosois sitting in his cell would ever have his door closed. But it was told of him how in the day of his sleeping, when the Fathers were sitting around him, his face shone like the sun, and he said to them, "Look, the abbot Anthony comes."[6] And after a little while, he said again to them, "Look, the company of the prophets comes." And again his face shone brighter, and he said, "Look, the company of the apostles comes." And his face shone with a double glory, and lo, he seemed as though he spoke with others. And the old men entreated him, saying, "With whom art thou speaking, Father?" And he said to them, "Behold, the angels came to take me, and I asked that I might be left a little while to repent." The old men said to him, "Thou hast no need of repentance, Father." But he said to them, "Verily I know not if I have clutched at the very beginning of repentance." And they all knew that he was made perfect. And again of a sudden his face was as the sun, and they all were in dread. And he said to them, "Look, behold the Lord cometh, saying, 'Bring me my chosen from the desert.'" And straightway he gave up the ghost. And there came as it might be lightning, and all the place was filled with sweetness.[7]

On the Transfiguration of the Body

On another Desert father St. Pambo, it is said; God so glorified him that no one could look at his face, because of the glory which his face had. (. . .) Just as Moses received the image of the glory of Adam, when his face was glorified, so the face of Abba Pambo shone like lightning, and he was as a king seated on his throne.[8]

---

5. Ibid., p. 177.

6. The text here refers to Anthony the Great (250-356), often called "the father of monastic life."

7. Ibid., pp. 180-181.

8. Quoted from Kallistos Ware, "The Transfiguration of the Body," p. 21.

Macarios of Egypt (ca. 300–ca. 390)

Homily 5, 8

The immaterial and divine fire illuminates the soul and puts it to the test. This fire descended on the apostles in the form of tongues of flame. This fire shone before Paul, it spoke to him, illuminated his mind and at the same time blinded his eyes, for the flesh cannot endure the brightness of this light. Moses saw this fire in the burning bush. This same fire lifted Elijah from the ground in the form of a flaming chariot. (...) This is the fire which pursues deamons and exterminates sins. It is the power of resurrection, the reality of eternal life, the illumination of holy souls, the stability of celestial powers.

Homily 1, 2

The soul becomes the "throne of God," it becomes altogether light, altogether a face, altogether an eye; each of its members filled with light, no place is left for darkness, as if it were full of spiritual eyes; on all sides it is a "face" turned toward God, receiving the light of Christ which enters within.

Homily 34, 1

But above all the eyes of the soul must be fixed on Christ, who, like a good painter, paints in those who believe in him and constantly behold him a portrait of the heavenly man, in His own image, by means of the Holy Spirit, out of the very substance of His ineffable light.[9]

Homily 5, 8

In so far as each has been counted worthy through faith and diligence to become a partaker of the Holy Spirit, to the same extent his body also shall be glorified in that day (the day of the resurrection). For what the soul has now stored up within, shall then be revealed and displayed outwardly in the body.

---

9. Macarios of Egypt, "Homily 34, 1," quoted after Vladimir Lossky, *Vision of God,* p. 115.

Homily 5, 9

At the day of resurrection the glory of the Holy Spirit comes out from within, decking and covering the bodies of the saints (. . .) the glory which they had before, but hidden within their souls. What a man has now, the same then comes forth externally in the body. (. . .) Their bodies shall be glorified through the unspeakable light which even now is within them (. . .) that is, the power of the Holy Spirit.

Gregory of Nazians (ca. 330–381)

Oration on Holy Baptism

God is Light: the highest, the unapproachable, the ineffable. . . . Moses' face was made glorious by it. And, to mention more lights — it was light that appeared out of fire to Moses, when it burned the bush indeed, but did not consume it. . . . And it was light that was in the pillar of fire that led Israel and tamed the wilderness. It was light that carried Elias in the car of fire. . . . It was light that shone round the shepherds. . . . It was light that was the beauty of the star that went before to Bethlehem to guide the wise men's way, and to be the escort of the Light that is above us, when He came amongst us. Light was that Godhead which was shown upon the mount to the disciples — and a little too strong for their eyes. Light was that vision which blazed out upon Paul, and by wounding his eyes healed the darkness of his soul. . . . Light beside these in a special sense is the illumination of baptism of which we are now speaking; for it contains a great and marvellous sacrament of our salvation.[10]

---

10. Nicene and Post-Nicene Fathers VII, 2nd Series, Gregory Naziansen, "Oration on Holy Baptism" p. 361.

Gregory of Nyssa (ca. 335–394),
Life of Moses

The Burning Bush

20   And if the flame by which the soul of the prophet was illuminated was kindled from a thorny bush, even this fact will not be useless for our inquiry. For if truth is God and truth is light — the Gospel testifies by these sublime and divine names to the God who made himself visible to us in the flesh — such guidance of virtue leads us to know that light which has reached down even to human nature. Lest one think that the radiance did not come from a material substance, this light did not shine from some luminary among the stars but came from an earthly bush and surpassed the heavenly luminaries in brilliance.[11]

21   From this we learn also the mystery of the Virgin: The light of divinity which through birth shone from her into human life did not consume the burning bush, even as the flower of her virginity was not withered by giving birth.

22   That light teaches us what we must do to stand within the rays of the true light: Sandaled feet cannot ascend that height where the light of truth is seen, but the dead and earthly covering of skins, which was placed around our nature at the beginning when we were found naked because of disobedience to the divine will, must be removed from the feet of the soul. When we do this, the knowledge of the truth will result and manifest itself. The full knowledge of being comes about by purifying our opinion concerning nonbeing.

23   In my view the definition of truth is this: not to have a mistaken apprehension of Being. Falsehood is a kind of impression which arises in the understanding about nonbeing: as though what does not exist does, in fact, exist. But truth is the sure apprehension of real Being. So, whoever applies himself in quietness to higher philosophical matters over a long period of

---

11. Gregory of Nyssa, *The Life of Moses,* 20, p. 59.

time will barely apprehend what true Being is, that is, what possesses existence in its own nature, and what nonbeing is, that is, what is existence only in appearance, with no self-subsisting nature.

24   It seems to me that at the time the great Moses was instructed in the theophany he came to know that none of those things which are apprehended by sense perception and contemplated by the understanding really subsists, but that the transcendent essence and cause of the universe, on which everything depends, alone subsists.

Eternal Progress

227   For this reason we also say that the great Moses, as he was becoming even greater, at no time stopped in his ascent, nor did he set a limit for himself in his upward course. Once having set foot on the ladder which God set up (as Jacob says), he continually climbed to the step above and never ceased to rise higher, because he always found a step higher than the one he had attained.

228   (. . .) He saw the brilliance of the light. Unencumbered, having taken off his sandals, he made his approach to the light.

229   He made camps under the cloud. He quenched thirst with the rock. He produced bread from heaven. By stretching out his hands, he overcame the foreigner. He heard the trumpet. He entered the darkness. He slipped into the inner sanctuary of the tabernacle not made with hands. He learned the secrets of the divine priesthood. He destroyed the idol. (. . .)

230   He shone with glory. And although lifted up through such lofty experiences, he is still unsatisfied in his desire for more. He still thirsts for that with which he constantly filled himself to capacity, and he asks to attain as if he had never partaken, beseeching God to appear to him, not according to his capacity to partake, but according to God's true being.

231   Such an experience seems to me to belong to the soul which loves what is beautiful. Hope always draws the soul from the beauty which is seen to what is beyond, always kindles the desire for the hidden through what is constantly perceived. Therefore, the ardent lover of beauty, although receiving what is always visible as an image of what he desires, yet longs to be filled with the very stamp of the archetype.

232   And the bold request which goes up the mountains of desire asks this: to enjoy the Beauty not in mirrors and reflections, but face to face. The divine voice granted what was requested in what was denied, showing in a few words an unmeasurable depth of thought. The munificence of God assented to the fulfillment of that desire, but did not promise any cessation or satiety of the desire.

233   He would not have shown himself to his servant if the sight were such as to bring the desire of the beholder to an end, since the true sight of God consists in this, that the one who looks up to God never ceases in that desire. For he says. "You cannot see my face, for man cannot see me and live" (Exod. 33:20).

234   Scripture does not indicate that this causes the death of those who look, for how would the face of life ever be the cause of death to those who approach it? On the contrary, the Divine is by its nature life-giving. Yet the characteristic of the divine nature is to transcend all characteristics. Therefore, he who thinks God is something to be known does not have life, because he has turned from true Being to what he considers by sense perception to have being.

235   True Being is true life. This Being is inaccessible to knowledge. If then the life-giving nature transcends all knowledge, that which is perceived certainly is not life. Thus, what Moses yearned for is satisfied by the very things which leave his desire unsatisfied.

236   He learns from what was said that the Divine is by its very nature infinite, enclosed by no boundary. If the Divine is perceived as though bounded by something, one must by all means consider along with that boundary what is beyond it. (...)

It is only logical that what encompasses is much larger than what is contained.

239 This truly is the vision of God: never to be satisfied in the desire to see him. But one must always, by looking at what he can see, rekindle his desire to see more. Thus, no limit would interrupt growth in the ascent to God, since no limit to the Good can be found nor is the increasing desire for the Good brought to an end because it is satisfied.

The Perfection of the Servant

318 Scripture describes another characteristic of this service to God: The eye is not dimmed nor does the person age. For how can an eye which is always in the light be dimmed by the darkness from which it is always separated? And the person who by every means achieves incorruption in his whole life admits no corruption in himself. For he has truly come to be an image of God and who has in no way turned aside from the divine character bears in himself its distinguishing marks and shows in all things his conformity to the archetype; he beautifies his own soul with what is incorruptable, unchangeable, and shares in no evil at all.

Conclusion

319 These things concerning the perfection of the virtuous life (. . .) we have briefly written for you, tracing in outline like a pattern of beauty the life of the great Moses so that each one of us might copy the image of the beauty which has been shown to us by imitating his way of life. (. . .)

320 Since the goal of the virtuous way of life was the very thing we have been seeking, and the goal has been found in what we have said, it is time for you, noble friend, to look to that example and, by transferring to your own life what is contemplated through spiritual interpretation of the things spoken literally, to be known by God and to become his friend. (. . .) we consider becoming God's friend the only thing worthy of honor and desire. This, as I have said, is the perfection of life.

On the Making of Man

As then painters transfer human forms to their pictures by means of certain colours, laying on their copy the proper and corresponding tints, so that the beauty of the original may be accurately transferred to the likeness, so I would have you understand that our Maker also, painting the portrait to resemble His own beauty, by the addition of virtues, as it were with colours, shows in us His own sovereignty: and manifold and varied are the tints, so to say, by which His true form is portrayed: not red, or white, or the blending of these, nor a touch of black that paints the eyebrow and the eye, and shades, by some combination (. . .), and all such arts which the hands of painters contrive, but instead of these, purity, freedom from passion, blessedness, alienation from all evil, and all those attributes of the like kind which help to form in men the likeness of God: with such hues as these did the Maker of His own image mark our nature.[12]

John Chrysostom (344-407)

Homily 56, Homilies on the Gospel of St. Matthew[13]

3. P. 346   But wherefore doth He bring forward Moses and Elias? One might mention many reasons. And first of all this: because the multitudes said He was, some Elias, some Jeremias, some one of the old prophets, He brings the leaders of His choir, that they might see the difference even hereby between the servants and the Lord; and that Peter was rightly commended and confessing Him Son of God. (. . .)

And one may mention another reason also. (. . .) Of what kind then is it? To inform them that He hath power both of death and life, is ruler both above and beneath. For this cause He brings forward both him that had died, and him that never yet suffered this.

But the fifth motive. (. . .) Now what was this? To show the glory of the cross, and to console Peter and the others in their dread of the passion, and

---

12. Nicene and Post-Nicene Fathers V, 2nd Series, Gregory of Nyssa, "On the Creation of Man," p. 391.

13. Nicene and Post-Nicene Fathers X, 1st Series, John Chrysostom, "On the Transfiguration," p. 391.

to raise up their minds, (. . .) and that they should be meek like Moses, and jealous for God like Elias, and full of tender care, as they were.

4. P. 347 What then saith the ardent Peter? "It is good for us to be here." For because he had heard that Christ was to go to Jerusalem and to suffer, being in fear still and trembling for Him, even after His reproof, he durst not indeed approach and say the same thing again, "Be it far from Thee" (Matt 16:22), but from that fear obscurely intimates the same again in other words. That is, when he saw the mountain, and so great retirement and solitude, his thought was, "He hath great security here. (. . .)" For he would have Him be there continually: wherefore also he speaks of "tabernacles." For, "if this might be," saith he, "we shall not go up to Jerusalem; and if we go not up, He will not die, for there He said the scribes would set upon Him."

But thus indeed he durst not speak; but desiring however to order things so, he said undoubtingly, "It is good for us to be here," where Moses also is present, and Elias; Elias who brought down fire on the mountain, and Moses who entered into the thick darkness, and talked with God; and no one will ever know where we are.

Seest thou the ardent lover of Christ? For look not now at this, that the manner of his exhortation was not well weighted, but see how ardent he was, how burning his affection to Christ.

(. . .) "If Thou wilt, let us make here three tabernacles, one for Thee and one for Moses, and one for Elias." What sayest thou, O Peter? didst thou not a little while since distinguish Him from the servants. Art thou again numbering Him with the servants? Seest thou how exceedingly imperfect they were before the crucifixion?

5. Pp. 348-349 What then? He Himself speaks nothing, nor Moses, nor Elias, but He that is greater than all, and more worthy of belief, the Father, uttereth a voice out of the cloud.

Wherefore out of the cloud? Thus doth God ever appear. "For a cloud and darkness are round about Him;" (Ps. 97:2) and, "He sitteth on a light cloud;" (Is. 19:1) and again, "Who maketh clouds His chariot;" (Ps. 104:3) and, "A cloud received Him out of their sight;" (Acts 1:9) and, "As the Son of Man coming in the clouds" (Dan. 7:13).

In order that they might believe that the voice proceeds from God, it comes from thence.

And the cloud was bright. For "while he yet spake, behold, a voice out of the cloud, which said, This is my beloved Son, in whom I am well pleased; hear ye Him" (Matt. 17:5).

For as, when He threatens, He shows a dark cloud; — as on Mount Sinai; for "Moses," it is said, "entered into the cloud, and into the thick darkness; and as a vapor, so went up the smoke" (Exod. 20:21, 19:18), and the prophet said, when speaking of His threatening, "Dark water in clouds of the air;" (Ps. 18:12) — so here, because it was His desire not to alarm, but to teach, it is a bright cloud.

And whereas Peter had said "Let us make three tabernacles," He showed a tabernacle not made with hands. Wherefore in that case it was smoke, and vapor of a furnace, but in this, light unspeakable and a voice.

(. . .)

And what saith the voice? "This is my beloved Son." Now if He is beloved, fear not Thou, O Peter.

(. . .)

"Hear ye Him." So that although He choose to be crucified, you are not to oppose Him.

6. P. 348 "And when they heard it, they fell on their face, and were sore afraid. (. . .) How then did they fall down on the mount (and not at the baptism of Christ)? Because there was solitude, and height, and great quietness, and a transfiguration full of awe, and a pure light, and a cloud stretched out; all which things put them in great alarm. And the amazement came thick on every side, and they fell down both in fear at once and in adoration.

7. 347 Nothing then is more blessed than the apostles, and especially the three, who even in the cloud were counted worthy to be under the same roof with the Lord.

But if we will, we also shall behold Christ, not as they then on the mount, but in far greater brightness. For not thus shall He come hereafter. For whereas then, to spare His disciples, He discovered so much only of His brightness as they were able to bear; hereafter He shall come in the very glory of the Father, not with Moses and Elias only, but with the infinite host of the angels, with the archangels, with the cherubim, with those infinite tribes, not having a cloud over His head, but even heaven itself being folded up.

(. . .)

"Then shall the righteous shine forth as the sun" (Matt. 13:43), or rather more than the sun. But so much is said, not because their light is to be so much and no more, but since we know no other star brighter than this, He chose by the known example to set forth the future brightness of the saints.

Pope Leo the Great (ca. 390–461)

Homily 51, On the Transfiguration[14]

I. P. 162   The Saviour of Mankind, Jesus Christ, (. . .) used to instruct His disciples by admonitory teaching and by miraculous acts to the end that He, the Christ, might be believed to be at once the Only-begotten of God and the Son of Man. For the one without the other was of no avail to salvation, and it was equally dangerous to have believed the Lord Jesus Christ to be either only God without manhood, or only man without Godhead, since both had equally to be confessed, because just as true manhood existed in His Godhead, so true Godhead existed in His manhood. To strengthen therefore, their most wholesome knowledge of this belief, the Lord had asked His disciples, among the various opinions of others, what they themselves believed, or thought about Him: whereat the Apostle Peter, by revelation of the most high Father passing beyond things corporeal and surmounting things human by the eyes of his mind, saw Him to be Son of the living God, and acknowledged the glory of the Godhead, because he looked not at the substance of His flesh and blood alone. (. . .)

II. P. 162   Jesus took Peter and James and his brother John, and ascending a very high mountain with them apart, showed them the brightness of His

---

14. Nicene and Post-Nicene Fathers XII, 2nd Series, Leo the Great, "Homily on the Transfiguration," p. 162.

glory; because, although they had recognised the majesty of God in Him, yet the power of His body, wherein His Deity was contained, they did not know.

III. P. 163   And in this Transfiguration the foremost object was to remove the offence of the cross from the disciples' heart, and to prevent their faith being disturbed by the humiliation of His voluntary passion by revealing to them the excellence of His hidden dignity.

IV. P. 163   For Moses and Elias, that is the Law and the Prophets, appeared talking with the Lord; that in the presence of those five men might most truly be fulfilled what was said: "In two or three witnesses stands every word" (Deut. 19:15). (. . .) For the pages of both covenants corroborate each other, and He Whom under the veil of mysteries the types that went before had promised, is displayed clearly and conspicuously by the splendour of the blessed glory. Because, as says the blessed John, "the Law was given through Moses: but the grace and truth came through Jesus Christ" (John 1:17).

V. Pp. 163-164   The Apostle Peter, therefore, being excited by the revelation of these mysteries, despising things mundane and scorning things earthly, was seized with a sort of frenzied craving for the things eternal, and being filled with rapture at the whole vision, desired to make his abode with Jesus in the place where he had been blessed with the manifestation of His glory. Whence also he says, "Lord, it is good for us to be here: if Thou wilt let us make three tabernacles, one for Thee, one for Moses, and one for Elias" (Matt. 17:4). But to this proposal the Lord made no answer, signifying that what was not indeed wicked, but contrary to the Divine order: since the world could not be saved, except by Christ's death.

VI. P. 164   The Father was indeed present in the Son, and in the Lord's brightness, which he had tempered to the disciples' sight, the Father's essence was not separated from the Only-begotten: but, in order to emphasize the two-fold personality, as the effulgence of the Son's body displayed the Son to their sight, so the Father's voice from out of the cloud announced the Father to their hearing.

VII. P. 164 Why tremble ye at being redeemed? Why fear ye to be healed of your wounds? Let that happen which Christ wills and I will.

Diadochos of Photiki (ca. 400–ca. 486)

On Spiritual Knowledge and Discrimination: One Hundred Texts[15]

§ 40 (P. 265) You should not doubt that the intellect, when it begins to be strongly energized by the divine light, becomes so completely translucent that it sees its own light vividly.

§ 59 (P. 270) Those who meditate unceasingly upon this glorious and holy name in the depths of their heart can sometimes see the light of their own intellect. For when the mind is closely concentrated upon this name, then we grow fully conscious that the name is burning up all the filth which covers the surface of the soul; for it is written: "Our God is a consuming fire" (Deut. 4:24).

§ 67 (P. 275) (The love of God's goodness) embraces our intellect with the light of the transforming fire, and so makes it a partner of the angels in their liturgy. Therefore, when we have been made ready, we begin to long sincerely for this gift of contemplative vision, for it is full of beauty, frees us from every earthly care, and nourishes the intellect with divine truth in the radiance of inexpressible light.

§ 80 (P. 281) The Logos of God chose to manifest the true light to creation through His own flesh, (and) with great compassion (He is) kindling the light of His holy knowledge within us.

§ 89 (P. 288) Divine grace confers on us two gifts through the baptism of regeneration, one being infinitely superior to the other. The first gift is given to us at once, when grace renews us in the actual waters of baptism

---

15. *The Philokalia*, Volume I, Diadochos of Photiki, *Spiritual Knowledge and Discrimination*, One Hundred Texts.

and cleanses all the lineaments of our soul, that is, the image of God in us, by washing away every stain of sin. The second — our likeness to God — requires our co-operation. When the intellect begins to perceive the Holy Spirit with full consciousness, we should realize that grace is beginning to paint the divine likeness over the divine image in us. Artists first draw the outline of a man in monochrome, and then add one colour after another, until little by little they capture the likeness of the subject down to the smallest details. In the same way the grace of God starts by remaking the divine image in man into what it was when he was first created. But when it sees us longing with all our heart for the beauty of the divine likeness and humbly standing naked in its atelier, then by making one virtue after another come into flower and exalting the beauty of the soul "from glory to glory" (2 Cor. 3:18), it depicts the divine likeness on the soul (. . .); but no one can acquire spiritual love unless he experiences fully and clearly the illumination of the Holy Spirit. If the intellect does not receive the perfection of the divine likeness through such illumination, although it may have almost every other virtue, it will still have no share in perfect love. (. . .) In portraiture, when the full range of colours is added to the outline, the painter captures the likeness of the subject, even down to the smile. Something similar happens to those who are being repainted by God's grace in the divine likeness: when the luminosity of love is added, then it is evident that the image has been fully transformed into the beauty of the likeness.

Dionysius the Areopagite (4-5th century)

The Celestial Hierarchies[16]

Father		
Son		I. Divine Triad
The Holy Spirit		
Seraphim		
Cherubim	1	
Thrones		
Dominions		
Virtues	2	II. The Angelic Hierarchy
Powers		
Principalities		
Archangels	3	
Angels		
Baptism		
The Eucharist	1	
Chrism		
Bishops		
Priests	2	III. Ecclesiastical Hierarchy
Deacons		
Monks		
Lay people	3	
Cathecumens		

Hierarchy is, in my opinion, a holy order and knowledge and activity which, so far as is attainable, participates in the Divine Likeness, and is lifted up to the illuminations given it by God, and correspondingly towards the imitation of God.[17]

16. Dionysius the Areopagite, *The Mystical Theology and The Celestical Hierarchies,* The Shrine of Wisdom.

17. *Celestial Hierarchies,* Chapter III, p. 29.

The Divine Names[18]

(. . .) when we have arisen incorruptible, immortal, and have attained the blessed Christ-like state, we shall be, as the Scripture says, "for ever with the Lord," filled, through the all-pure and holy contemplations, with the visible manifestation of God Himself, shining through us with most radiant splendour, as about the disciples in the Transfiguration. And so, in the degree that the mind is freed from passion and the things of the world, we shall participate in His intelligible Light and we shall be united to Him in the union above intellect, through the unknown and most blessed brilliance of those dazzling Rays.[19]

For the light comes forth from the Good and is an image of goodness; wherefore the Good is celebrated under the Name of Light, just as the archetype is manifested by the image.

(. . .) so, too, the great sun, wholly bright and ever-shining — the manifested image and a feeble echo of the Divine Goodness — both illuminates all that can receive its light whilst itself preserving its exempt unity, and unfolds to the visible universe above and below the splendour of its own rays. And if anything does not participate in them, this is not because of any weakness or deficiency in its distribution of light, but rather is due to an inaptitude for the reception of the light on the part of those things which do not open themselves to receive it.

(. . .)

Let us now celebrate the intelligible Name of Light given to the Good, and declare that He who is the Good is called Intellectual or Spiritual Light because He fills all the Celestial Minds with super-celestial Light and drives out from all souls whatsoever ignorance and error there may be within them, and imparts to them all His holy Light and purifies their intellectual sight from the mist in which their ignorance envelops them, and energizes and opens the eyes that were closed through the great weight of darkness, and bestows at first a tempered radiance; then when they taste the light as it were and desire more, He gives it in greater measure and shines upon them more abundantly because they have loved much, and ever uplifts them to things beyond, according to their power of gazing upward.

---

18. Dionysius the Areopagite, *The Divine Names,* The Shrine of Wisdom.
19. *The Divine Names,* Chapter I, p. 12.

(. . .)

For just as ignorance disperses those who have gone astray, so the presence of spiritual Light accomplishes the unification of those whom It enlightens, perfects them, and converts them towards That which truly is by drawing them away from a multitude of opinions and collecting their various views — or to speak precisely, notions — into one true, pure and uniform knowledge and filling them with unitive and unifying Light.[20]

Mystical Theology

Leave behind the senses and the operations of the intellect, and all things sensible and intellectual (. . .) that thou mayest arise by unknowing (agnosia) towards the union (henosis), as far as attainable, with him who transcends all being and all knowledge. For by the unceasing and absolute renunciation of thyself and of all things thou mayest be borne on high, through pure and entire self-abnegation, into the superessential radiance of the divine darkness.[21]

It was not without reason that the blessed Moses was commanded first to undergo purification himself and then to separate himself from those who had undergone it; and after the entire purification heard many-voiced trumpets and saw many lights streaming forth with pure and manifold rays, and that he was thereafter separated from the multitude, with the elect priests, and pressed forward to the summit of the divine ascent. Nevertheless, he did not attain to the presence of God himself; he saw not him (for he cannot be looked upon) but the place where he dwells. And this I take to signify that the divinest and highest things seen by the eyes and contemplated by the mind are but the symbolical expressions of those that are immediately beneath him who is above all. Through these, his incomprehensible presence is manifested upon those heights of his holy places (. . .) and plunges the mystic into the darkness of unknowing, whence all perfection of understanding is excluded, and he is enwrapped in that which is altogether intangible and noumenal, being wholly absorbed in him who is beyond all, (. . .) and through the inactivity of all his reasoning powers is united by his highest faculty to him who is wholly unknowable.[22]

20. Ibid., Chapter IV, pp. 32-34.
21. *Mystical Theology,* Chapter I, p. 9.
22. Ibid., p. 11.

Maximos the Confessor (580-662)
Two Hundred Texts on Theology[23]

First Century

§ 97 (P. 134)   To the more diligent students of Holy Scripture the Lord is clearly shown as having two forms. The first is common and more popular, and it can be perceived by many. The text "We saw Him and He had no comeliness or beauty" (Is. 53:2) refers to this form. The second is more hidden, and it can be perceived only by a few, that is, by those who have already become like the holy apostles Peter and John, before whom the Lord was transfigured with a glory that overwhelmed the senses (Matt. 17:2). The text "Thou art fairer than the children of men" (Ps. 45:2) refers to this form. The first of these two forms is consonant to beginners; the second to those perfected in spiritual knowledge, in so far as such perfection is possible. The first is an image of the Lord's initial advent, to which the literal meaning of the Gospel refers, and which by means of wisdom transfigures and deifies those imbued with spiritual knowledge: because of the transfiguration of the Logos within them "they reflect with unveiled face the glory of the Lord" (2 Cor. 3:18).

Second Century

§ 13 (P. 140)   For the Lord does not always appear in glory to all who stand before Him. To beginners He appears in the form of a servant (Phil. 2:7), to those able to follow Him as He climbs the high mountain of His transfiguration He existed before the world came to be (John 17:5). (. . .) (He appears) according to the measure of each person's faith.

§ 14 (Pp. 140-141)   When the Logos of God becomes manifest and radiant in us, and His face shines like the sun, then His clothes will also look white (Matt. 17:2). That is to say, the words of the Gospels will then be clear and distinct, with nothing concealed. And Moses and Elijah — the more

23. *The Philokalia,* Volume II, *Two Hundred Texts on Theology and the Incarnate Dispensation of the Son of God.*

spiritual principles of the Law and the prophets — will also be present with Him.

§ 15 (P. 141)   (. . .) the Logos of God is transfigured to the degree to which each has advanced in holiness. (. . .) For the more spiritual principles in the Law and the prophets — symbolized by Moses and Elijah when they appeared with the Lord at His transfiguration — manifest their glory according to the actual receptive capacity of those to whom it is revealed.

§ 16 (P. 141)   These tabernacles represent three stages of salvation, namely that of virtue, spiritual knowledge and theology. The first requires fortitude and self-restraint in the practice of the virtues: of this type was Elijah. The second requires right discernment in natural contemplation: Moses discloses this in his own person. The third requires the consummate perfection of wisdom: this was revealed by the Lord. They were called tabernacles, or temporary dwellings, because beyond them there are other still more excellent and splendid stages, through which those found worthy will pass in the age to be.

§ 28 (P. 144)   before His visible advent in the flesh the Logos of God dwelt among the patriarchs and prophets in a spiritual manner, prefiguring the mysteries of His advent. After His incarnation He is present in a similar way not only to those who are beginners (. . .), but also to the perfect, secretly pre-delineating in them the features of His future advent as if in an ikon.

§ 39 (P. 147)   If you theologize in an affirmative or cataphatic manner, starting from positive statements about God, you make the Logos flesh, for you have no other means of knowing God as cause except from what is visible and tangible. If you theologize in a negative or apophatic manner, through the stripping away of positive attributes, you make the Logos spirit or God as He was in His principal state with God: starting from absolutely none of the things that can be known, you come in an admirable way to know Him who transcends unknowing.

§ 76 (P. 156)   The Apostle Paul says that he had a partial knowledge of the

Logos (1 Cor. 13:9). The Evangelist John states that he has seen His glory: "For we beheld His glory," he says, "the glory as of the only-begotten Son of the Father, full of grace and truth" (John 1:14). Perhaps St. Paul says that he has but a partial knowledge of the divine Logos because the Logos is known from His energies only to a limited degree, while knowledge of Him as He is in essence and person is altogether inaccessible to all angels and men alike.

(. . .) For "when He appears," says Scripture, "we shall be like Him" (1 John 3:2).

§ 80 (P. 158)   He who has made his heart pure (. . .), he will in some measure see God himself. (. . .) When God comes to dwell in such a heart, he honours it by engraving his own letters on it by the Holy Spirit, just as he did on the Mosaic tablets (Exodus 31:18). This he does according to the degree to which the heart, through practice of the virtues and contemplation, has devoted itself to the admonition which bids us, in a mystical sense, "Be fruitful and multiply!" (Gen. 1:28).

§ 82 (P. 158)   A pure heart is one which offers the mind to God free of all image and form, and ready to be imprinted only with His own archetypes, by which God Himself is made manifest.

§ 88 (P. 160)   For the body is deified along with the soul through its own corresponding participation in the process of deification. Thus God alone is made manifest through the soul and the body, since their natural properties have been overcome by the superabundance of His glory.

John Climacus (ca. 579–ca. 649)

The Ladder of Divine Ascent[24]

P. 74   A Christian is an imitator of Christ in thought, word and deed, as far as this is humanly possible. (. . .) The monk has a body made holy, a tongue purified, a mind enlightened.

24. John Climacus, *The Ladder of Divine Ascent,* The Classics of Western Spirituality.

P. 75 Those of us who wish to get away from Egypt, to escape from Pharaoh, need some Moses to be our intermediary with God, to stand between action (praxis) and contemplation (theoria). (Moses as prototype of a spiritual father.)

P. 143 The depths of mourning (over sin) have witnessed comfort, and enlightenment has followed on purity of heart. Enlightenment is something indescribable, an activity (energy) that is unknowingly perceived and invisibly seen.

P. 178 I do not think anyone should be classed as a saint until he has made holy his body, if indeed that is possible.

P. 195 The truly obedient monk often becomes suddenly radiant and exultant during his prayers.

P. 223 No one of us can describe the power and nature of the sun. We can merely deduce its intrinsic nature from its characteristics and effects. So too with humility, which is a god-given protection against seeing our own achievements.

(...) You will know that you have this holy gift within you (...) when you experience an abundance of unspeakable light together with an indescribable love of prayer.

P. 242 (...) for the perfect there is increase and, indeed, a wealth of divine light.

(...) The sun is bright when clouds have left the air; and a soul, freed of its old habits and also forgiven, has surely seen the divine light.

P. 249 There is the way of stillness and the way of obedience. And in addition to these there is the way of rapture, the way of the mind mysteriously and marvelously carried into the light of Christ.

P. 270 Let the remembrance of Jesus be present with your every breath. Then indeed you will appreciate the value of stillness (hesychia).

P. 274 Prayer is by nature a dialog and a union of man with God.

P. 280 It is one and the same fire that is called that which consumes (Heb. 12:29) and that which illuminates (John 1:9). Hence the reason why some emerge from prayer as from a blazing furnace and as though having been relieved of all material defilements. Others come forth as if they were resplendent with light and clothed in a garment of joy and of humility.

P. 288 For when the heart is cheerful, the face beams (Prov. 15:13), and a man flooded with the love of God reveals in his body, as if in a mirror, the splendour of his soul, a glory like that of Moses when he came face to face with God (Exod. 34:29-35).

P. 248 There is one thing about us that never ceases to amaze me. Why is it that when we have almighty God, the angels, and the saints to help us toward virtue, and when only the devil is against us, we still incline so readily to the passions? (...) how is it, as the great Gregory (of Nazianzus) puts it, that I am the image of God, yet mingled with clay? Is it not a fact that a creature of God that has strayed from its created nature will continuously try to return to its original condition? Indeed everyone should struggle to raise his clay, so to speak, to a place on the throne of God.

P. 284 I long for the undying beauty that you gave me before this clay.

Pp. 250-251 But there is no boundary to virtue. The psalmist says, "I have seen the end of all perfection, but Your commandment is very broad and is without limit" (Ps. 118:96) (...), and if it is true that love never fails (1 Cor. 13:8), (...) then love has no boundary, and both in the present and in the future age we will never cease to progress in it, as we add light to light. (...) even the angels make progress and indeed they add glory to glory and knowledge to knowledge.

John of Damascus (ca. 675–ca. 749)
On the Divine Images[25]

First Apology

4, Pp. 15-16   I do not adore the creation rather than the Creator, but I adore the one who became a creature, who was formed as I was, who clothed Himself in creation without weakening or departing from His divinity, that He might raise our nature in glory and make us partakers of His divine nature (2 Pet. 1:4). Together with my King, my God and Father, I worship Him who clothed Himself in the royal purple of my flesh. (. . .)

Therefore I boldly draw an image of the invisible God, not as invisible, but as having become visible for our sakes by partaking of flesh and blood. I do not draw an image of the immortal Godhead, but I paint the image of God who became visible in the flesh.

5, Pp. 16-17   "The Lord spoke to you out of the midst of the fire; you heard the sound of words but saw no form; there was only a voice" (Deut. 4:12). And shortly thereafter: "Take good heeds to yourselves. Since you saw no form on the day that the Lord spoke to you at Horeb out of the midst of the fire, beware lest you act corruptly by making a graven image for yourself, in the form of any figure, the likeness of male or female, the likeness of any beast that is on the earth, or the likeness of any bird that flies in the air" (Deut. 4:15-17). And again, "Beware lest you lift up your eyes to heaven, and when you see the sun and the moon and the stars, all the host of heaven, you be drawn away and worship them and serve them" (Deut. 4:19).

7, P. 17   You see that He forbids the making of images because of idolatry, and that it is impossible to make an image of the immeasurable, uncircumscribed, invisible God. For "You heard the sound of words, but saw no form; there was only a voice" (Deut. 4:12).

---

25. John of Damascus, *On the Divine Images,* Three Apologies against Those Who Attack the Divine Images.

8, P. 18 These commandments were given to the Jews because of their proneness to idolatry. (...) "You cannot see my form (My face)," Scripture says (Exod. 33:20). What wisdom the Lawgiver has! How can the invisible be depicted? How does one picture the inconceivable? How can one draw what is limitless, immeasurable, infinite? How can a form be given to the formless? How can you describe a mystery? It is obvious that when you contemplate God becoming man, then you may depict Him clothed in human form. When the invisible One becomes visible to flesh, you may then draw His likeness.

16, Pp. 23-25 In former times God, who is without form or body, could never be depicted. But now when God is seen in the flesh conversing with men, I make an image of the God who is seen in the flesh conversing with men, I make an image of the God whom I see. I do not worship matter; I worship the Creator of matter who became matter for my sake, who willed to take his abode in matter; who worked out my salvation through matter. Never will I cease honoring the matter which wrought my salvation. I honor it, but not as God.

(. . .) Was not the thrice-happy and thrice-blessed wood of the cross matter? (...) Is not the ink in the most holy Gospel-book matter? Is not the life-giving altar made of matter? From it we receive the bread of life! Are not gold and silver matter? From them we make crosses, patens, chalices! And over and above all these things, is not the Body and Blood of our Lord matter? Either do away with the honor and veneration these things deserve, or accept the tradition of the Church and the veneration of images. (...) Do not despise matter, for it is not despicable. God has made nothing despicable. To think such things is Manichaeism. Only that which does not have its source in God is despicable — that which is our own invention, our willful choice to disregard the law of God — namely, sin.

(. . .) If you invoke the law in your despising of images, you might as well insist on keeping the sabbath and practicing circumcision.

17, P. 25 We use all our senses to produce worthy images of Him, and we sanctify the noblest of the senses which is that of sight. For just as words edify the ear, so also the image stimulates the eye. What the book is to the literate, the image is to the illiterate. Just as words speak to the ear, so the image speaks to the sight; it brings us understanding.

18, P. 26   Through Him, human nature rose from the lowest depths to the most exalted heights, and in Him sat on the Father's throne.

21, Pp. 28-29   St. Basil says, "the honor given to the image is transferred to its prototype."
(. . .) From the time that God the Word became flesh, He is like us in everything except sin, and partakes of our nature without mingling or confusion. He has deified our flesh forever, and has sanctified us by surrendering His Godhead to our flesh without confusion.

22, P. 30   I have seen God in human form and my soul has been saved.

Commentary

P. 40   If according to common parlance the honor due the image is transferred to the prototype, as holy Basil says, why should we not bow down to honor the image, not as God, but as the image of God incarnate?

Second Apology

5, P. 52   But we are not mistaken if we make the image of God incarnate, who was seen on earth in the flesh, associated with men, and in His unspeakable goodness assumed the nature, feeling, form and color of our flesh. For we yearn to see how He looked, as the apostle says, "Now we see through a glass darkly" (1 Cor. 13:12). Now the icon is also a dark glass, fashioned according to the limitations of our physical nature.

11, P. 58   If anyone should dare to make an image of the immaterial, bodiless, invisible, formless, and colorless Godhead, we reject it as falsehood.

16, P. 63   The Manichaeans wrote the Gospel according to Thomas; will you now write the Gospel according to Leo? (Leo III, iconoclastic emperor).

20, P. 65   "Now we see in a mirror dimly" (1 Cor. 13:12), in the image, and thus we are blessed. God Himself first made an image, and presented images to our sight, for "God created (the first) man in His own image" (Gen. 1:27), and Abraham, Moses, Isaiah, and all the prophets saw images of God, but not the essence of God. The burning bush was an image of God's Mother, and when Moses was about to approach it, God said, "Do not come near; put off your shoes from your feet, for the place on which you are standing is holy ground" (Exod. 3:5). Now if the ground where Moses saw an image of the Theotokos is holy ground, how much more holy is the image itself?

Third Apology

12, Pp. 72-73   The apostles saw Christ in the flesh; they witnessed His sufferings and His miracles, and heard His words. We too desire to see, and to hear, and so be filled with gladness. They saw Him face to face, since He was physically present, we hear His words read from books and by hearing our souls are sanctified and filled with blessings, and so we worship, honoring the books from which we hear His words. So also, through the painting of images, we are able to contemplate the likeness of His bodily form, His miracles, and His passion, and thus are sanctified, blessed and filled with joy. Reverently we honor and worship His bodily form, and by contemplating His bodily form, we form a notion, as far as it is possible for us, of the glory of His divinity. Since we are fashioned by both soul and body, and our souls are not naked spirits, but are covered, as it were, with a fleshly veil, it is impossible for us to think without using physical images. Just as we physically listen to perceptible words in order to understand spiritual things, so also by using bodily sight we reach spiritual contemplation. For this reason Christ assumed both soul and body, since man is fashioned from both. Likewise baptism is both of water and of Spirit. It is the same with communion, prayer, psalmody, candles, or incense; they all have a double significance, physical and spiritual.

What is an image?

16, Pp. 73-74   An image is a likeness, or a model, or a figure of something, showing in itself what it depicts. An image is not always like its prototype in every way. For the image is one thing, and the thing depicted is another; one can always notice differences between them, since one is not the other, and vice versa.

17, P. 74 All images reveal and make perceptible those things which are hidden. (. . .) Therefore, images are a source of profit, help, and salvation for all, since they make things so obviously manifest, enabling us to perceive hidden things. Thus, we are encouraged to desire and imitate what is good and to shun and hate what is evil.

How many kinds of images are there?

18, Pp. 74-75 First we have a human being; only then can we have words and pictures. The Son of the Father is the first natural and precisely similar image of the invisible God, for He reveals the Father in His own person. "No one has ever seen God" (John 1:18). (. . .) The Apostle says that the Son is the image of the Father: "He is the image (eikon) of the invisible God" (Col. 1:15), and to the Hebrews he says, ". . . who, being the brightness of His glory and the image of His substance" (Heb. 1:3). (. . .) The Son is the natural image of the Father, precisely similar to the Father in every way, except that He is begotten by the Father, who is not begotten.

20, P. 76 The third kind of image is made by God as an imitation of Himself: namely, man. How can what is created share the nature of Him who is uncreated, except by imitation?

Who first made images?

26, Pp. 80-81 In the beginning He who is God begot His only Son, His Word, the living image of Himself, the natural and precisely similar likeness of His eternity. And He made man after His own image and likeness (Gen. 1:26). (. . .)

God did not unite Himself with angelic nature, but with human nature. God did not become an angel; He became a man by nature and in truth. (. . .) Angels do not share in this; they do not become partakers of the divine nature. But by the operation of grace, men do share in and become partakers of the divine nature, as many of them as receive the holy Body of

Christ and drink His Blood, since His person is united with the Godhead, and the two natures of Christ's Body which we eat are inseparably joined in His person.

What are the different ways we offer this relative worship to created things?

33, P. 84   First of all, those places where God, who alone is holy, has rested. He rests in holy places: that is, the Theotokos, and all the saints. These are they who have become likenesses of God as far as possible, since they have chosen to cooperate with divine election. Therefore God dwells in them. They are truly called gods, not by nature, but by adoption, just as red-hot iron is called fiery, not by its nature, but because it participates in the action of the fire. (. . .)

We do not back away and refuse to touch red-hot iron because of the nature of the iron, but because it has partaken of what is hot by nature. The saints are to be venerated because God has glorified them. (. . .)

37, P. 87   The fifth kind of relative worship is our veneration of each other, since we are God's inheritance, and were made according to His image, and so we are subject to each other, thus fulfilling the law of love.

41, P. 89   We venerate images; it is not veneration offered to matter, but to those who are portrayed through matter in the images. All honor given to an image is transferred to its prototype, as St. Basil says.

Cyril of Jerusalem, from the twelfth catechetical instruction

P. 102   He called all creation good, but only men were made in His image. The sun came into existence by only a command, but man was fashioned by His own divine hands.

Appendix

Symeon the New Theologian (949-1022)
The Discourses[26]

The Vision of the Light

Pp. 245-246 One day, as he stood and recited, "God, have mercy upon me, a sinner," uttering it with his mind rather than his mouth, suddenly a flood of divine radiance appeared from above and filled all the room. As this happened the young man lost all awareness (of his surroundings) and forgot that he was in a house or that he was under a roof. He saw nothing but light all around him and did not know if he was standing on the ground. (. . .) Instead, he was wholly in the presence of immaterial light and seemed to himself to have turned into light. Oblivious of all the world he was filled with tears and ineffable joy and gladness. His mind then ascended to heaven and beheld yet another light, which was clearer than that which was close at hand. In a wonderful manner there appeared to him, standing close to that light, the saint of whom we have spoken, the old man equal to angels (Symeon's spiritual father).

The Light and the Ecstasy

Pp. 200-201 I fell prostrate to the ground, and at once I saw, and behold, a great light was immaterially shining on me and seized hold of my whole mind and soul, so that I was struck with amazement at the unexpected marvel and I was, as it were, in ecstasy. Moreover, I forgot the place where I stood, who I was, and where, and could only cry out, "Lord, have mercy," so that when I came to myself I discovered that I was reciting this. "But Father," said he, "who it was that was speaking, and who moved my tongue, I do not know — only God knows." "Whether I was in the body, or outside the body" (2 Cor. 12:2-3), I conversed with this Light. The Light itself knows it; it scattered whatever mist there was in my soul and cast out every earthly care. It expelled from me all material denseness and bodily heaviness that made my members to be sluggish and numb. What an awesome mar-

---

26. Symeon the New Theologian, *The Discourses,* The Classics of Western Spirituality.

vel! It so invigorated and strengthened my limbs and muscles, which had been faint through great weariness, that it seemed to me as though I was stripping myself of the garment of corruption. Besides, there was poured into my soul in unutterable fashion a great spiritual joy and perception and a sweetness surpassing every taste of visible objects, together with a freedom and forgetfulness of all thoughts pertaining to this life. In a marvelous way there was granted to me and revealed to me the manner of the departure from this present life. Thus all the perceptions of my mind and my soul were wholly concentrated on the ineffable joy of that Light.

The Enjoyment of Such a Light

Pp. 201-202   "But tell me, (. . .) what were the effects of what you have seen?" (. . .) "Father, when it appears it fills one with joy, when it vanishes it wounds. It happens close to me and carries me up to heaven. (. . .) The light envelops me and appears to me like a star, and it is incomprehensible to all. It is radiant like the sun, and I perceive all creation encompassed by it. It shows me all that it contains, and enjoins me to respect my own limits. I am hemmed in by roof and walls, yet it opens the heavens to me. (. . .) I hear a voice speaking to me secretly from on high, "These things are but symbols and preliminaries, for you will not see that which is perfect as long as you are clothed in the flesh. But return to yourself and see that you do nothing that deprives you of the things that are above. Should you fall, however, it is to recall you to humility!

From the Shadow of the Law to the Light of God

P. 298   It shines on us without evening, without change, without alteration, without form. It speaks, works, lives, gives life, and changes into light those whom it illuminates. We bear witness that "God is light," and those to whom it has been granted to see Him have all beheld Him as light. Those who have received Him have received Him as light, because the light of His glory goes before Him, and it is impossible for Him to appear without light.

Knowledge Is Not the Light

P. 301 Knowledge is not the light! Rather, it is the light that is knowledge, since "in it and through it and from it are all things" (Rom. 11:36).

The Need for Kindling the Lamp of the Soul

P. 339 God is fire (Heb. 6:4) and He is so called by all the inspired Scripture (Heb. 12:29). The soul of each of us is a lamp. Now a lamp is wholly a darkness, even though it be filled with oil or tow or other combustible matter, until it receives fire and is kindled. So too the soul, though it may seem to be adorned with all virtues, yet does not receive the fire — in other words, has not received the divine nature and light — and is still unkindled and dark and its works are uncertain. All things must be tested and manifested by the light (Eph. 5:13).

For Having Taken Hold of God in His Simplicity

P. 365 As we ascend to that which is more perfect, He who is without form or shape comes no longer without form or without shape. (. . .) He comes in a definite shape indeed, though it is a divine one. Yet God does not show Himself in a particular pattern or likeness, but in simplicity, and takes the form of an incomprehensible, inaccessible, and formless light. (. . .) He appears clearly and is consciously known and clearly seen, though He is invisible. He sees and hears invisibly and, just as friend speaks to friend face to face (Exod. 33:11), so He who by nature is God speaks to those whom by grace He has begotten as gods.

For a Rapture into Glory

P. 373 Thou didst vouchsafe to show me Thy face in the heavens above, as if they were rent apart (Acts 7:56). It was a light like the sun without form.

For a Vision before the Icon of the Theotokos

P. 376 I longed to see Thee again. I went off to reverence the spotless ikon of her who bore Thee. As I fell before it, before I rose up, Thou Thyself didst appear to me within my poor heart, as though Thou hadst transformed it into light; and then I knew that I have Thee consciously within me.

Gregory the Sinaiite (ca. 1265–1346)

Discourse on the Transfiguration[27]

4 For type stood to type, in each case, in a relationship of greater perfection; thus was the darkness related to the light, and Horeb to Thabor. (...)

Therefore (on Horeb) terrible light and sight of the back and unapproachable darkness and vision of fire (...) were there meted out. But here on Thabor the same God shone ineffably and appeared lovingly and auspiciously to us men.

6 But behold: the darkness there (on Horeb) symbolised the light, and the cloud symbolised the cloud of the Spirit here (on Thabor); the fire symbolised the purification; the trumpet was the loud-speaker of the Word of God; the thunder-claps symbolised the preaching. There there were flashes of lightning, while here there was divine illumination surpassing the sun (...); the things which took place there were used by Him prophetically as patterns, one may say, and as a paedagogic model. (...) (He is) at once light and the cause of light (...), for He is, and is called, Light above cause and reason.

7 (...) He made that display of light there on the mountain and came into their view, His purpose was to show both the splendour of the glory to come and the pure beauty of the incarnation, by which God became truly man in a super-human way.

9 And Elijah the fire-bringer, recognising the God who came in fire and

27. Gregory the Sinaiite, *Discourse on the Transfiguration,* translated by David Balfour, Athens 1982.

breath, perceiving Him whom he had previously beholden flashing forth now on Thabor more brightly than the sun, and astonished by the unexpectedness of the vision and of their timeless meeting, probably wished to sharpen his zeal against the disobedient, but was held back by this joy overcoming his anger.

10   (. . .) Moses and Elijah, having been seen both together with Jesus long ago — (the one) in the darkness and (the other) in the light — should also stand by Him (now). (. . .) The prophets were declaring either the long-suffering meekness (of Moses) and the zeal (of Elijah), or the two natures of the Word. (. . .)

12   As they gazed at Him, suddenly His countenance shone brighter than the sun and His raiment became dazzling and white as the light. And astonished in mind and overcome by the divine light, they fell to the earth, one on his back, the other face downward, oppressed by the brightness which welled out from the fount of light; and as though encompassed, they were frozen to the spot. But Peter woke up and perceived His glory, amazed at the frightening nature of the unexpected sight; and in his consternation, seeing the two men, Moses and Elijah, standing together at his side, he said to Jesus, "Master, it is good for us to be here" and then "Let us make three tabernacles, one for each," not knowing what he was saying, his mind being in a state of entrancement and inebriation.

13   For when the mind is swallowed up by that ineffable light and becomes separated from the world of things, it is deprived of the sensual perception of relationships and (God) dims the very senses by the light of His power: or contrariwise, by the light He separates the mind from the senses and the senses from relationships and causes it to be possessed by divine love, repelling every sensual attachment of the mind to things perceptible.

17   For as has been said, the darkness was a type of the transfiguration. Now both have gone by, but the transfiguration is the truth of that theophany which is present in each, while again the latter is an earnest of the eternal beatitude in the other world and partakes in the ineffable outpouring of light, when we shall be transfigured in one light and glory, becoming

eternal, and be made snow-white from above on the spiritual (Mount) Selmon of inconceivable peace, as is written, by the thearchic light, and shall revolve round the outpourings of radiance, singing as we dance.

18   And they feared, says the evangelist, "when they entered into the cloud," and a voice came out of the cloud, saying: "This is My beloved Son, in whom I am well pleased." For then truly did the unlimited Lord Jesus thunder from the mountain as from heaven in the storm of light and the sound of the glory of His coming; and the Father in the highest raised His voice, a voice of power from out of the shining cloud, saying, as is written, to the disciples:

"This is my beloved Son, the only begotten, transfigured on Thabor to-day in His human nature. He is the very image of My substance, the efful-gence of My glory, the immutable likeness of My superessentiality. (. . .) He is the light that was begotten. I am the source of the light; He is life, I am the cause of the life. (. . .) In the light of His glory you shall see Me, the unap-proachable light. In Him you shall recognise Me and in Me you shall see Him.

23   By our formula of prayer ("Lord Jesus Christ, have mercy on me a sin-ner"), we give expression in the Spirit to the word that "no man can say, Je-sus is Lord, unless in the Holy Spirit." He be invoked. He is heard by the ears of our soul, leaping in our heart and "making intercession for us" to the Father "with groanings which cannot be uttered" (Rom. 8:26).

24   And as the Son shone ineffably on Thabor in the light of his power, they clearly discerned the Father of lights through that voice from above and the Spirit through the resplendent cloud, and recognised the Trinity as an everlasting outpouring of light and brightness, truly flashing forth like lightning in the transfigured Christ. Then even the mountains rejoiced and were glad — as is said, "Thabor and Hermon rejoice in Thy name," — and heaven exulted and all the earth leapt with joy, seeing on the mountain their own master shining more brightly than the sun both sensibly and intelligi-bly, and illuminating and sanctifying all things. (. . .) The powers, looking down from above, shuddered; and the earth, from below, trembled with joy and fear. Thus all creation, all nature, "every thing that hath breath" praised, glorified and magnified Him, seeing its master and king, who had shown through previously as founder, as creator, now transfigured and transformed on the mountain and resplendent beyond the sun as God. (. . .)

25   Let us observe with Moses and ascend together with Elijah; let us enquire into divine matters with John and confess our acknowledgement with Peter and approach the light with James, and let us gaze, in so far as possible, on his "glory as of the only begotten from the Father" (John 1:14).

Gregory Palamas (1296-1359)
The Triads[28]

C. The Hesychast method of prayer, and the transformation of the body

I.ii.1, P. 41   (. . .) How can it be that God at the beginning caused the mind to inhabit the body? Did even he do ill? Rather, brother, such views befit the heretics, who claim that the body is an evil thing, a fabrication of the Wicked One. As for us, we think that the mind becomes evil through dwelling on fleshly thoughts, but that there is nothing bad in the body, since the body is not evil in itself.

(. . .) "I am sold to sin," Paul says (Rom. 7:14). But he who is sold is not a slave by nature.

3, Pp. 42-43   (. . .) Some place the mind in the brain, as in a kind of Acropolis; others hold that its vehicle is the very centre of the heart. (. . .) "For it is from the heart that evil thoughts come" (Matt. 15:19). And the great Macarius says also, "The heart directs the entire organism, and when grace gains possession of the heart, it reigns over all the thoughts and all the members; for it is there, in the heart, that the mind and all the thoughts of the soul have their seat."

(. . .) Macarius immediately goes on to say, "It is there one must look to see if grace has inscribed the laws of the Spirit." Where but in the heart, the

---

28. Gregory Palamas, *The Triads,* The Classics of Western Spirituality.

controlling organ, the throne of grace, are the mind and all the thoughts of the soul to be found?

Can you not see, then, how essential it is that those who have determined to pay attention to themselves in inner quiet should gather together the mind and enclose it in the body, and especially in that "body" most interior to the body, which we call the heart?

4, Pp. 43-44   Do you not see that if one desires to combat sin and acquire virtue, (. . .) one must force the mind to return within the body and oneself?

5, P. 44   Has it not occurred to them that the mind is like the eye, which sees other visible objects but cannot see itself? (. . .) This is what the great Denys calls the movement of the mind "along a straight line"; and on the other hand, it returns upon itself, when it beholds itself; this movement the same Father calls "circular." This last is the most excellent and most appropriate activity of the mind, by which it comes to transcend itself and be united to God. "For the mind," says St. Basil, "which is not dispersed abroad, returns to itself, and through itself mount towards God."

7, P. 45   On the other hand, it is not out of place to teach people, especially beginners, that they should look at themselves, and introduce their own mind within themselves through control of breathing. (. . .) for those newly approaching this struggle find that their mind, when recollected, continually becomes dispersed again. It is thus necessary for such people constantly to bring it back once more; but in their inexperience, they fail to grasp that nothing in the world is in fact more difficult to contemplate and more mobile and shifting than the mind.

8, Pp. 46-47   How should such a one not gain great profit if, instead of letting his eye roam hither and thither, he should fix it on his breast or on his navel, as a point of concentration? For in this way, he will not only gather himself together externally, conforming as far as possible to the inner movement he seeks for his mind; he will also, by disposing his body in such a position, recall into the interior of the heart a power which is ever flowing outwards through the faculty of sight.

9, Pp. 47-48   For just as those who abandon themselves to sensual and corruptible pleasures fix all the desires of the soul upon the flesh, and indeed become entirely "flesh," (. . .) so too, in the case of those who have elevated their minds to God and exalted their souls with divine longing, participating together with the soul in the divine communion, and becoming itself a dwelling and possession of God; for it is no longer the seat of enmity towards God, and no longer possesses desires contrary to the Spirit.

II.ii.5, P. 48   For this body which is united to us, has been attached to us as a fellow-worker by God, or rather placed under our control. Thus we will repress it, if it is in revolt, and accept it, if it conducts itself as it should.

6, P. 49   For (. . .) if we cannot taste mental prayer, (. . .) and if we are dominated by passionate emotions, then we certainly stand in need of the physical suffering that comes from fasting, vigils and similar things, (. . .) and according to Gregory the Theologian, "God heals in no more certain way than through suffering." This is why the Lord taught us in the Gospels that prayer can do great things when combined with fasting (Matt. 17:21, Mark 9:29).

12, P. 52   The soul, since it experiences divine things, doubtless possesses a passionate part, praiseworthy and divine: or rather; there is within us a single passionate aspect which is capable of thus becoming praiseworthy and divine. (. . .)

What of Stephen, the first martyr, whose face, even while he was yet living, shone like the face of an angel? Did not his body also experience divine things?

19, P. 54   It is thus not the man who has killed the passionate part of his soul who has preeminence, (. . .) the prize goes to him who has put that part of his soul under subjection, so that by its obedience to the mind, which is by nature appointed to rule, it may ever tend towards God, as is right, by the uninterrupted remembrance of Him. Thanks to this remembrance, he will come to possess a divine disposition, and cause the soul to progress towards the highest state of all, the love of God.

20, P. 55   Our tongues, our hands and feet must likewise be at the service of the Divine Will. Is it not such a practice of the commandments of God a common activity of body and soul, and how can such activity darken and blind the soul?

D. Deification in Christ (theosis)

II.iii.9, P. 57 . . . This light is not the essence of God, for that is inaccessible and incommunicable. (. . .) Sometimes it makes a man go out from the body or else, without separating him from the body, it elevated him to an ineffable height. At other times, it transforms the body, and communicates its own splendour to it when, miraculously, the light which deifies the body becomes accessible to the bodily eyes. Thus indeed did the great Arsenius appear when engaged in hesychastic combat; similarly Stephen, whilst being stoned, and Moses, when he descended from the mountain.

12, P. 59 But why should one consider the essence of God as a light of this kind? None of us has ever defined a contemplative as one who has seen the divine essence!

16, P. 61 (. . .) let us have faith in Him who has participated in our nature and granted it in return the glory of His own nature, and let us seek how to acquire this glory and see it. How? By keeping the divine commandments. For the Lord has promised to manifest Himself to the man who keeps them. (. . .)

17, P. 62 But we also know that the fulfillment of the commandments of God gives true knowledge, since it is through this that the soul gains health. How could a rational soul be healthy, if it is sick in its cognitive faculty? So we know that the commandments of God also grant knowledge, and not that alone, but deification also.

18, P. 63 Indeed, this light of contemplation even differs from the light that comes from the holy Scriptures, whose light may be compared to "a lamp that shines in an obscure place," whereas the light of mystical contemplation is compared to the star of the morning which shines in full daylight, that is to say, to the sun.

20, Pp. 63-64   But the enemies of such illumination and such a light also claim that all the lights which God has manifested to the saints are only symbolic apparitions, allusions to immaterial and intelligible realities, shown forth in the imagination through God's providence in particular circumstances, falsely alleging that St. Denys the Areopagite is in agreement with them. In fact the latter states quite clearly that the light which illuminated the disciples at the most holy Transfiguration will continually and endlessly dazzle us "with its most brilliant rays" in the Age to Come, when we will be "always with the Lord."

(...) Shall we say that this light, the beauty of the eternal Age to Come, is only a symbol, an illusion, something without true existence? Certainly not, as long as we remain lovers of this light.

33, P. 64   In respect of its transcendence, it might better be called ignorance than knowledge. (...) This union, then, is a unique reality. For whatever name one gives to it — union, vision, sense perception, knowledge, intellection, illumination — would not, properly speaking, apply to it, or else would properly apply to it alone.

35, P. 65   "The end of prayer is to be snatched away to God" (John Climacus). This is why the great Denys says that through prayer, we are united to God. For in prayer, the mind gradually abandons all relation with created things: first with all things evil and bad, then with neutral things capable of conformity to either good or ill, according to the intentions of the person using them. It is to this last category that all studies belong and the knowledge that comes through them. (...) This ecstasy is incomparably higher than negative theology. (...) But it is not yet union, unless the Paraclete illumines from on high. (...)

36, Pp. 65-66   But I am incapable of expressing and explaining these matters. (...) But is the union with this light other than a vision?

For it is in light that the light is seen, and that which operates in a similar light, since this faculty has no other way in which to work. Having separated itself from all other beings, it becomes itself all light and is assimilated to what it sees, or rather, it is united to it without mingling, being itself light and seeing light through light. If it sees itself, it sees light; if it looks at the means by which it sees, again it is light. For such is the character of the union, that all is one, so that he who sees (...) simply has the awareness of being light and of seeing a light distinct from every creature.

37, P. 66 This is why the great Paul after his extraordinary rapture declared himself ignorant of what it was. Nonetheless, he saw himself. (...) He was that to which he was united. (...)

Paul therefore was light and spirit, to which he was united. (...) But in attaining this condition, the divine Paul could not participate absolutely in the divine essence. (...)

68, P. 69 But those who possess not only the faculties of sensation and intellection, but have also obtained spiritual and supernatural grace, do not gain knowledge only through created things, but also know spiritually, in a manner beyond sense and intelligence, that God is spirit, for they have become entirely God, and know God in God. It is therefore by this mystical knowledge that divine things must be conceived, as the same St. Denys reminds us, and not by natural faculties. We must transcend ourselves altogether, and give ourselves entirely to God, for it is better to belong to God, and not to ourselves.

E. The uncreated Glory

III.i.10, P. 72 "The blessed Moses, by virtue of the glory of the Spirit which shone on his face, and which no man could bear to gaze upon, showed by this sign how the bodies of the saints would be glorified after the resurrection of the righteous. (...)"

(...) "The glory which even now enriches the souls of the saints will cover and clothe their naked bodies after the resurrection, and will elevate them to the heavens, clad in the glory of their good deeds and of the Spirit; that glory which the souls of the saints have received now in part. (...) Thus, glorified by the divine light, the saints will be always with the Lord" (Macarius of Egypt).

According to the great Denys, that was the same light which illumined the chosen apostles on the Mountain: "When we become incorruptible and immortal," he says, "and attain to the blessed state of conformity with

Christ, we will ever be with the Lord, as Scripture says (1Thess. 4:17), gaining fulfillment in the purest contemplations of His visible theophany, just as it illuminated the disciples at the time of the most divine Transfiguration."

(. . .) As Gregory the Theologian remarked, "In my view, he will come as he appeared or was manifested to the disciples on the Mountain, the divine triumphing over the corporeal."

11, Pp. 72-73 "But," Barlaam says, "this light was a sensible light, visible through the medium of the air, appearing to the amazement of all and then at once disappearing. One calls it 'divinity' because it is a symbol of divinity."

(. . .)

Why in the Age to Come should we have more symbols of this kind, more mirrors, more enigmas? Will the vision face-to-face remain still in the realm of hope? For indeed if even in heaven there are still to be symbols, mirrors, enigmas, then we have been deceived in our hopes, deluded in sophistry; thinking that the promise will make us acquire the true divinity, we do not even gain a vision of divinity. A sensible light replaces this, whose nature is entirely foreign to God! How can this light be a symbol, and if it is, how can it be called divinity?

12, P. 73 What saint has ever said that this light was a created symbol?

12, P. 74 Again, Basil the Great, after showing that the God Who is adored in three Persons is a unique light, speaks of the "God who dwells in light unapproachable." (. . .) This is why the apostles fell to the ground, unable to rest their gaze on the glory of the light of the Son, because it was a "light unapproachable." The Spirit, too, is light, as we read: "He who has shone in our hearts by the Holy spirit" (2 Cor. 4:6).

(. . .) This is why we sing together to the Lord when we celebrate the annual Feast of the Transfiguration: "In Your light which appeared today on Thabor, we have seen the Father as light and also the Spirit as light," for "You have unveiled an indistinct ray of Your divinity." . . . So, when all the saints agree in calling this light true divinity, how do you dare to consider it alien to the divinity, calling it "a created reality," and "a symbol of divinity," and claiming that it is inferior to our intellection?

15, P. 76 Indeed, not only will Christ be eternally thus in the future, but He was such even before He ascended the Mountain. Hear John Damascene, who is wise in divine things: "Christ is transfigured, not by putting on some quality He did not possess previously, nor by changing into something He never was before, but by revealing to His disciples what He truly was, in opening their eyes and in giving sight to those who were blind. For while remaining identical to what He has been before, He appeared to the disciples in His splendour; He is indeed the true light, the radiance of glory."

(. . .) And do not the annual hymns of the Church affirm that, even before the Transfiguration, He had previously been such as He then appeared? "What appeared today was hidden by the flesh, and the original beauty, more than resplendent, has been unveiled today."

Moreover, the transformation of our human nature, its deification and transfiguration — were these not accomplished in Christ from the start, from the moment in which he assumed our nature? (. . .) This light, then, was not a hallucination but will remain for eternity, and has existed from the beginning.

16, Pp. 76-77 All then must follow and obey Him Who says, "Come, let us ascend the holy and heavenly mountain, let us contemplate the immaterial divinity of the Father and the Spirit, which shines forth in the only Son" (John of Damascus, Canon II for the Feast of the Transfiguration).

Macarius similarly states, "Our mixed human nature, which was assumed by the Lord, has taken its seat on the right hand of the divine majesty in the heavens, being full of glory not only (like Moses) in the face, but in the whole body."

19, P. 78 This light cannot pertain to His human nature, for our nature is not light, let alone a light such as this. The saviour did not ascend Thabor, accompanied by the chosen disciples, in order to show them that He was a man. (. . .) No, He went up to show them "that He was the radiance of the Father" (Heb. 1:3).

22, P. 80 (. . .) This mysterious light, inaccessible, immaterial, uncreated, deifying, eternal, this radiance of the Divine Nature, this glory of the divinity, this beauty of the heavenly kingdom, is at once accessible to sense perception and yet transcends it. Does such a reality really seem to you to be a symbol alien to divinity, sensible, created and "visible through the medium of the air"?

Listen again to Damascene's assertion that the light is not alien but natural to the divinity. "The splendour of divine grace is not something external, as in the case of the splendour possessed by Moses, but belongs to the very nature of the divine glory and splendour."

(...) the fact that it is not visible through the medium of air shows us it is not a sensible light. Indeed, when it was shining on Thabor more brilliantly than the sun, the people of the area did not even see it! ...

23, P. 81 (...) we have learnt to sing together to Christ: "The chosen disciples were transformed by the divine ecstasy on the Mountain, contemplating the irresistible outpouring of Your light and Your unapproachable Divinity."

You might as well claim that God is a creature, as declare that His essential energies are created! For no intelligent man would say that the essential goodness and life are the superessential essence of God. The essential characteristic is not the essence which possesses the essential characteristics. (...) Similarly, the deifying light is also essential, but is not itself the essence of God.

26, P. 82 You claim that the grace of deification is a natural state, that is, the activity and manifestation of a natural power. Without realising it, you are falling into the error of the Messalians, for the deified man would necessarily be God by nature, if deification depended on our natural powers, and was included among the laws of nature!

(...) Deification would then be a work of nature, not a gift of God, and the deified man would be god by nature and receive the name of "God" in the proper sense.

27, P. 83 The grace of deification thus transcends nature, virtue and knowledge. (...) Every virtue and imitation of God on our part indeed prepares those who practise them for divine union, but the mysterious union itself is effected by grace. (...) So, when you hear that God dwells in us through the virtues, or by the means of the memory He comes to be established in us, do not imagine that deification is simply the possession of the virtues; but rather that it resides in the radiance and grace of God, which really comes to us through the virtues.

32, P. 87 Deification is in fact beyond every name. This is why we, who have written much about hesychia (. . .) have never dared hitherto to write about deification.

33, P. 88 For, as the Apostle says, "In Christ the fulness of the divinity dwells bodily" (Col. 2:19).

This is why certain saints after the Incarnation have seen this light as a limitless sea, flowing forth in a paradoxical manner from the unique Sun, that is, from the adorable Body of Christ, as in the case of the apostles on the Mountain.

F. Essence and energies in God

7, Pp. 95-96 The wise Maximus (the Confessor) thus rightly says that "existence, life, holiness and virtue are works of God that do not have a beginning in time," (and) "There was never a time when virtue, goodness, holiness and immortality did not exist." (. . .)

Therefore, neither the uncreated goodness, nor the eternal glory, nor the divine life nor things akin to these are simply the superessential essence of God, for God transcends them all as Cause. But we say He is life, goodness and so forth, and give Him these names, because of the revelatory energies and powers of the Superessential. (. . .)

But since God is entirely present in each of the divine energies, we name Him from each of them, although it is clear that He transcends all of them.

11, P. 98 Denys the Areopagite says, "If we call the superessential Mystery 'God' or 'Life' or 'Essence' or 'Light' or 'Word,' we are referring to nothing other than the deifying powers which proceed from God and come down to us, creating substance, giving life, and granting wisdom."

14, P. 100 Moreover, every union is through contact, sensible in the realm of sense perception, intellectual in that of intellect. And since there is union with these illuminations, there must be contact with them, of an intellectual, or rather spiritual, kind. As for the divine essence, that is in itself beyond all contact.

Now, this union with illuminations — what is it, if not a vision? The rays are consequently visible to those worthy, although the divine essence is absolutely invisible, and these unoriginate and endless rays are a light without beginning or end. (. . .)

This spiritual light is thus not only the object of the vision, but it is also the power by which we see; it is neither a sensation nor an intellection, but is a spiritual power, distinct from all created cognitive faculties in its transcendence, and made present by grace in rational natures which have been purified.

9, P. 106 We do not see distant objects as if they were in front of our eyes, nor the future as if it were the present; we do not know the will of God concerning us before it comes to be. Yet the prophets knew the designs of God which eternally preexisted in God, even before they were accomplished. Similarly, the chosen disciples saw the essential and eternal beauty of God on Thabor (as the Church sings) . . . not the glory of God which derives from creatures, as you think, but the superluminous splendour of the beauty of the Archetype, the very formless form of the divine loveliness, which deifies man and makes him worthy of personal converse with God, eternal and endless, the very light beyond intellection and unapproachable, the heavenly and infinite light, out of time and eternal, the light that makes immortality shine forth, the light which deifies those who contemplate it.

10, P. 107 Do you not see that these divine energies are in God, and remain invisible to the created faculties? Yet the saints see them, because they have transcended themselves with the help of the Spirit.

Do you not understand that the men who are united to God and deified, who fix their eyes in a divine manner on Him, do not see as we do? Miraculously, they see with a sense that exceeds the senses, and with a mind that exceeds mind, for the power of the spirit penetrates their human faculties, and allows them to see things which are beyond us. (. . .)

You fail to understand that God's inner being is not at all the same as an existent object, and you imagine wrongly that the things around God — the natural attributes appertaining to Him — are identical with His inner being.

11, P. 108 For one applies the word "sun" to the rays as well as to the source of the rays; yet it does not follow that there are two suns. There is, then, a single God, even though one says that the deifying grace is from God. The light is also one of the things that "surround" the sun, yet it is certainly not the essence of the sun. So how could the light which shines from God upon the saints be the essence of God?

13, Pp. 109-110 How then do we know this light is also deification? Listen to the same Father (Maximus the Confessor). Having explained as far as possible the way in which deified men are united to God — a union akin to that of the soul and the body, so that the whole man should be entirely deified, divinised by the grace of the incarnate God — he concludes: "He remains entirely man by nature in his soul and body, and becomes entirely God in his soul and body through grace, and through the divine radiance of the blessed glory with which he is made entirely resplendent. Do you note that this light is the radiance of God? Is the radiance of God then created?

14, P. 110 But they (the Fathers) tell us that God transcends all else "an infinite number of times," since they know that His transcendence is inexpressible by any thought or word whatsoever.

BIBLIOGRAPHY

The Apocalypse of Peter, The Ante-Nicene Fathers, Volume X, edited by Allan Menzies, Eerdmans, Grand Rapids, Michigan 1969.

Athanasios av Alexandria, *Antonios liv,* Tomas Hägg och Samuel Rubenson, Artos Bokförlag, Skellefteå 1991.

Diadochos of Photiki, Spiritual Knowledge and Discrimination, One Hundred Texts, in *The Philokalia,* Volume I, Faber and Faber, London Boston 1986 (1979).

Dionysius the Areopagite, *The Divine Names,* The Shrine of Wisdom, Surrey 1980.

Dionysius the Areopagite, *The Mystical Theology and The Celestial Hierarchies,* The Shrine of Wisdom, Surrey 1965.

Dionysius of Fourna, *The Painter's Manual,* translated by Paul Hetherington, The Sagittarius Press, London 1974.

Documents of the Christian Church, selected and edited by Henry Bettenson, Second Edition, Oxford University Press, Oxford New York Toronto Melbourne 1979 (1943).

Eusebius Pamphili, *Life of Constantine the Great,* The Nicene and Post-Nicene Fathers, Second Series, Volume I, edited by Philip Schaff and Henry Wace, Eerdmans, Grand Rapids, Michigan 1961 (1890).

The Festal Menaion & The Lenten Triodion, Faber and Faber, London Boston 1984 (1978), translated by Mother Mary and Archimandrite Kallistos Ware.

Gregory of Nyssa, *The Life of Moses,* The Classics of Western Spirituality, Paulist Press, New York Ramsey Toronto 1978.

Gregory Palamas, *The Triads,* The Classics of Western Spirituality, Paulist Press, New York Ramsey Toronto 1983.

Gregory the Sinaiite, *Discourse on the Transfiguration,* translated by David Balfour, Athens 1982.

The Holy Bible, Revised Standard Version, Catholic Edition, Ignatius Press, San Francisco 1966.

John Chrysostom, *Homilies on the Gospel of St. Matthew,* The Nicene and Post-Nicene Fathers, First Series, Volume X, edited by Philip Schaff, Eerdmans, Grand Rapids, Michigan 1987 (1888).

John Climacus, *The Ladder of Divine Ascent,* The Classics of Western Spirituality, Paulist Press, New York Ramsey Toronto 1982.

John of Damascus, *On the Divine Images,* Three Apologies against Those Who Attack the Divine Images, St. Vladimir's Seminary Press, New York 1980.

Leo the Great, *The Letters and Sermons,* The Nicene and Post-Nicene Fathers, Second Series, Volume XII, edited by Philip Schaff and Henry Wace, Eerdmans, Grand Rapids, Michigan 1983 (1890).

Maximos the Confessor, *Two Hundred Texts on Theology and the Incarnate Dispensation of the Son of God,* in *The Philokalia,* Volume II, Faber and Faber, London Boston 1990 (1981).

Origen of Alexandria, *Commentary on the Gospel of Matthew,* The Ante-Nicene Fathers, Volume X, edited by Allan Menzies, Eerdmans, Grand Rapids, Michigan 1969.

The Philokalia, Volume I, Faber and Faber, London Boston 1986 (1979).

The Philokalia, Volume II, Faber and Faber, London Boston 1990 (1981), translated and edited by G. E. H. Palmer, Philip Sherrard and Kallistos Ware.

Symeon the New Theologian, *The Discourses,* The Classics of Western Spirituality, Paulist Press, New York Ramsey Toronto 1980.

Theodore the Studite, *On the Holy Icons,* St. Vladimir's Seminary Press, New York 1981.

Arseniev, Nicholas, *Mysticism in the Eastern Church,* St. Vladimir's Seminary Press, Crestwood, New York 1979 (1926).

Baggley, John, *Doors of Perception — Icons and Their Spiritual Significance,* Mowbray, Oxford & London 1987.

Bibliography

Baxandall, Michael, *Painting and Experience in Fifteenth Century Italy,* Oxford University Press, Oxford New York 1985 (1972).

Bloom, Anthony, "Body and Matter in Spiritual Life," in *Sacrament and Image, Essays in the Christian Understanding of Man,* edited by A. M. Allchin Fellowship of St. Alban and St. Sergius, London 1987 (1967) pp. 36-46.

Bodin, Per-Arne, *Världen som ikon,* Artos Bokförlag, Skellefteå 1987.

Bodin, Per-Arne, *Den oväntade glädjen,* Artos Bokförlag, Skellefteå 1991.

Børtnes, Jostein, *Visions of Glory,* Solum Forlag A/S, Oslo 1988.

Cormack, Robin, *Writing in Gold, Byzantine Society and Its Icons,* George Philip, London 1985.

Danbolt, Gunnar, *Noen trekk fra alterutsmykningens historie,* Foreningen til norske fortidsminnesmerkers bevaring, Oslo 1986, s. 13-44.

Danbolt, Gunnar, and Siri Meyer, *Når bilder formidler,* Universitetsforlaget, Oslo 1988.

Demus, Otto, *Byzantine Mosaic Decoration, Aspects of Monumental Art in Byzantium,* Caratzas Brothers, Publishers, New Rochelle, New York 1976 (1948).

Duckett, Eleanor, *Death and Life in the Tenth Century,* Ann Arbor, The University of Michigan Press 1968.

Forsyth, George, and Kurt Weitzmann, *The Monastery of Saint Catherine at Mount Sinai, The Church and Fortress of Justinian,* The University of Michigan Press 1973.

Frost, Tore, and Egil A. Wyller (redaksjon), *Gresk Åndsliv, Fra Homer til Elytis,* Tanum-Norli, Oslo 1983.

Frye, Northrop, *The Great Code,* The Bible and Literature, Harcourt Brace Jovanovich, Publishers, New York and London 1982 (1981).

Gendle, Nicholas, *Creation and Incarnation in the Iconology of St. John of Damascus,* A Festschrift for Archbishop Methodius of Thyateira and Great Britain, Aten 1985.

Gillet, Lev, A Monk of the Eastern Church, *The Jesus Prayer,* St. Vladimir's Seminary Press, Crestwood, New York 1987.

Ihm, Christa, *Die Programme der christlichen Apsismalerei von vierten Jahrhundert bis zur Mitte des achten Jahrhunderts,* Wiesbaden 1960.

Kitzinger, Ernst, *The Art of Byzantium and the Medieval West: Selected Studies,* ed. W. E. Kleinbauer, Indiana University Press, Bloomington London 1976.

Lossky, Vladimir, *The Mystical Theology of the Eastern Church,* James Clarke, Cambridge London 1973 (1957).

Lossky, Vladimir, *The Vision of God,* St. Vladimir's Seminary Press, New York 1983 (1963).

Mango, Cyril, *The Art of the Byzantine Empire, 312-1453, Sources and Documents,* in the series Sources and Documents in the History of Art, edited by H. W. Janson, Prentice-Hall, Englewood Cliffs, New Jersey 1972.

Mantzaridis, Georgios I., *The Deification of Man, St. Gregory Palamas and the Ortodox Tradition,* St. Vladimir's Seminary Press, New York 1984.

Merton, Thomas, *The Wisdom of the Desert,* Darley Anderson, The Anchor Press, London 1974 (1961).

Meyendorff, John, *A Study of Gregory Palamas,* The Faith Press, Beds 1974 (1964).

Meyendorff, John, *Byzantine Theology, Historical Trends and Doctrinal Themes,* Fordham University Press, New York 1976 (1974).

Nordström, Carl-Otto, *Ravennastudien,* Almquist & Wiksell, Stockholm 1953.

Onasch, Konrad, *Die Ikonenmalerei,* Koehler & Amelang, Leipzig 1967.

Onasch, Konrad, *Kunst und Liturgie der Ostkirche in Stichworten,* Koehler & Amelang, Leipzig 1981.

Ouspensky, Leonid, *Theology of the Icon,* St. Vladimir's Seminary Press, New York 1978.

Ouspensky, Leonid, and Vladimir Lossky, *The Meaning of Icons,* St. Vladimir's Seminary Press, Crestwood, New York 1982 (1952).

Panofsky, Erwin, *Meaning in the Visual Arts,* Penguin Books, Singapore 1983 (1955).

Payne, Robert, *The Holy Fire, The Story of the Fathers of the Eastern Church,* St. Vladimir's Seminary Press, Crestwood, New York 1980 (1957).

Pelikan, Jaroslav, *The Christian Tradition, A History of the Development of Doctrine,* Volume 2, *The Spirit of Eastern Christendom (600-1700),* The University of Chicago Press, Chicago and London 1974.

Rubenson, Samuel, *Ett odelat hjärta, En studie i ökenfädernas vishet,* Artos Bokförlag, Skellefteå 1984.

Sahas, Daniel J., *Icon and Logos, Sources in Eighth-Century Iconoclasm,* University of Toronto Press, Toronto Buffalo London 1988 (1986).

Schiller, Gertrud, *Ikonographie der Christlicher Kunst I,* Gütersloher Verlagshaus, Gütersloh 1966.

Bibliography

Simson, Otto G. von, *Sacred Fortress, Byzantine Art and Statecraft in Ravenna,* The University of Chicago Press, Chicago 1948.

Skard, Bjarne, *Inkarnasjonen, En dogmehistorisk fremstilling,* Gyldendal Norsk Forlag, Oslo 1976 (1951).

The Study of Spirituality, edited by Cheslyn Jones, Geoffrey Wainwright, Edward Yarnold, S.J., SPCK, London 1986.

Torp, Hjalmar, *The Integrating System of Proportion in Byzantine Art,* Acta Volume IV, Rome 1984.

Waddell, Helen, *The Desert Fathers,* Constable, London 1987 (1931).

Ward, Benedicta, *The Wisdom of the Desert Fathers,* SLG Press, Oxford 1986 (1975).

Ward, Benedicta, *The World of the Desert Fathers,* SLG Press, Oxford 1986.

Ware, Kallistos, "The Transfiguration of the Body," in *Sacrament and Image, Essays in the Christian Understanding of Man,* edited by A. M. Allchin, Fellowship of St. Alban and St. Sergius, London 1987 (1967) pp. 19-35.

Weitzmann, Kurt, *Studies in the Arts of Sinai,* Princeton University Press, Princeton, New Jersey 1982.